Guided Meditations for Children

40 Scripts and Activities Based on the Sunday Lectionary

Sydney Ann Merritt

Resource Publications, Inc.
San Jose, California

Editorial director: Kenneth Guentert
Managing editor: Elizabeth J. Asborno

Front cover illustration by George Collopy.

Reprint Department
Resource Publications, Inc.
160 E. Virginia Street #290
San Jose, CA 95112-5876

Library of Congress Cataloging in Publication Data
Merritt, Sydney Ann.
    Guided meditations for children : 40 scripts and activities based on the Sunday lectionary / Sydney Ann Merritt.
        p.   cm.
    ISBN 0-89390-336-1
    1. Church year meditations. 2. Children—Prayer-books and devotions—English. [1. Church year. 2. Prayer books and devotions. 3. Meditation.] I. Title.
    BV4870.M445 1995
    242'.3—dc20   94-48152

Printed in the United States of America

99 98 | 5 4 3 2

To the memory of my daughter, Colleen Marie.
I shall miss you always.

Contents

Part I: Advent & Christmas

Part II: Lent & Easter

Part III: Ordinary Time

Acknowledgments

Special thanks to my husband, Lee, and to my children; my parents, Howard and Louise Ross; my second "Mom," Lillian Leonard; my wonderful grandchildren, who inspired me; and to all my family and friends who made this project possible.

Teaching Children to Experience Jesus through Prayer

The meditations presented in this book are an effective method of teaching children how to experience Jesus within themselves—in their minds and hearts. The meditations follow the church seasons and are based on the lectionary gospel readings for cycles A, B, and C. At the beginning of each meditation, I list the related scripture citation, Sunday and season (with cycle[s] indicated in parentheses), and suggested background music.

This book speaks to the spiritual lives of children, teaching children to establish a place in their imaginations where they can be with Jesus at any time or place. Meditations evoke children's vivid imaginations, leading them to their own experience of Jesus and spirituality. The meditations meet a child's uncomplicated and direct way of understanding the word of God. The children are led into a Gospel scene where they will encounter the Lord through touch, feel, love, and prayer. They will "hear" the brush of angels' wings, experience the wonderment and joy on the day of Pentecost, and feel the coolness of the water as they step into the Jordan River with Jesus.

The meditations can be merged into any religious education program. For those who use CELEBRATING THE LECTIONARY

1

from Resource Publications, Inc., you can incorporate the meditations into your weekly lesson plan as an alternate activity or use them as introductions or conclusions to a unit.

Quiet time and group discussion questions follow each meditation. I do not suggest inviting the children to share their own experience of the meditation because this should remain a personal time with Jesus. However, if children volunteer to share their experiences, you will find this stimulating to the discussion time.

Suggestions for Success

Teaching children to experience Jesus through prayer should be rewarding spiritually for the presenter as well as for the children. Following a few simple suggestions will help to insure your success.

To Begin

Begin with "A Place to Meet," the introductory guided meditation found at the end of this introduction. This will create a place in the children's imagination to meet Jesus.

Personal Reflection

Before presenting a meditation, take a few minutes for your personal reflection on the gospel scene. What images quicken your imagination? Ask yourself, "What is Jesus saying to me?"

Practice

To help you become more comfortable with this form of prayer, practice reading the meditation aloud slowly just as you will with the children. You may choose to record and play back the meditation, listening for pauses and voice inflection. Are you speaking too softly or too quickly? Are you pausing long enough? Remember:

- Read slowly with slight pauses where indicated (....). For longer pauses, wait 35-40 seconds or until you notice the children becoming restless.
- Avoid speaking in a monotone. Change your voice to emphasize a change in character or scene.

Music

Background music is very important; it sets the tone and helps activate the imagination. You will find music suggestions at the beginning of each meditation. (See "Music Resources" for listing of suggested recorded music.) Don't be afraid to experiment with your own favorite instrumental. Live music and sounds—soft guitar strumming, gentle piano music, tinkling wind chimes—can also be helpful.

Space

Give some thought to how you will create an atmosphere of prayer for the children.

- Lower the lights or pull the shades.
- Use a candle.
- Create a focal point by combining important elements: an open bible; a candle; natural objects like rocks, driftwood, or greenery; other items of significance to the children.

Make sure the children will be physically comfortable. Is the room too hot or too cold? Some children may prefer sitting in their own seat or sitting on the floor rather than lying on the floor. Floor pillows or carpet squares are a great way of indicating private space.

Too Many Wiggles

Initially, before children are used to guided meditations, you may need to use a gentle form of discipline to keep the wiggling and whispering from getting out of hand.

- Remind children that this is a time to be with Jesus and not to bother their neighbor.
- Establish direct eye contact with the wiggler. This may suffice. If necessary, walk within reach of the disruptive child, touch him/her on the shoulder, and whisper "Shhh."
- Changing the place of one child can often quiet the entire room.
- Include the child's name in the meditation, for example, "Jesus notices that Danny is not listening. He places a gentle hand on Danny's shoulder and whispers, 'Shhh.'"
- Be ready to shorten or rephrase a meditation, depending on the age of the children and their attention span. Some may be too long or have too much detail for young children.

Discussion

Allow time for discussion questions. Invite response, but do not demand participation.

Keep Trying

Do not become discouraged if your first attempts are not what you hoped for. Even your first awkward attempts will have an impact. Each child will take home something different after his/her visit with Jesus.

4

The Meeting Place

Suggested Music: "Peace Is Flowing Like a River"/*Gentle Sounds*

Sometimes I get so busy I don't take time to listen for Jesus' voice. This is not good for me. I have learned my life seems to go much better when I remember to say, "Good morning, Jesus," and to thank Jesus just before I go to sleep. Sometimes, at night, I just try to listen for his voice. Have you ever tried this? Sometimes Jesus speaks to people like me and you through a tiny voice called a conscience. At times I find it difficult to talk to Jesus because I cannot see him. Do you have that problem? (*Allow time for discussion.*)

There is a way we can see Jesus. It is called our imaginations. Do you ever use your imaginations when you are playing? Imagining people, places, and things? Is there a special place that you like to go to in your imagination? Where would you like to meet Jesus? (*Allow time for discussion.*) Maybe we could try something right now.

Have children move apart, either stretched out on the floor or sitting comfortably. Ask them to unzip their imaginations and close their eyes. This is their private time to talk to Jesus and to listen to Jesus in their hearts. Take time to relax them with your voice, getting them to breathe deeply and slowly and to relax their bodies. Play the suggested background music to help set the mood.

Meditation

Close your eyes....Shrug your shoulders....Take a deep
breath....Let it out slowly....Whisper "Jesus"....Relax....

Imagine that you are walking down a dusty path on a warm
spring day and you pass by a tall man with long hair....In
the background you can hear water washing against the
sandy shore....The man turns to speak to you....Can you
see him?....It is Jesus!...."Where are you going, Lord?" you
ask....Jesus smiles....He takes your hand in his....Feel his
gentle touch...."Come follow me," he answers....You and
Jesus walk hand in hand toward the water....Jesus sits on
the ground with his back resting against an olive tree....
Look into his eyes....Jesus looks toward the blue-green
lake....He stands, inviting you to walk with him to the
water's edge....Be careful going down the sloping earth....
"Don't fall," Jesus cautions....Jesus dips his hand into the
cool water, forms a cup with his hand, then offers you a
drink....Taste the fresh cold water....Jesus dips his hand into
the water once again....Playfully, he splashes cold droplets
of water on your bare feet....Shiver with the cold....You and
Jesus laugh....Splash Jesus back....Isn't nice to laugh with
Jesus?....

Taking Jesus by the hand, lead him to your favorite place....

Tall trees line the path, reaching their arms to the heavens
....Birds fly from branch to branch....Take a deep breath....
The air smells sweet of fresh grass and rose blossoms....
Look up at the sky....Clouds slowly drift across the face of
the sun....A warm breeze blows Jesus' hair....You are now
at your special place....It may be at home, in a park, high in
the mountains, or on a sandy beach....You can be with
Jesus wherever you want to be....Invite Jesus to sit down....
Sit beside him or perhaps on his lap....No one will see you
....Feel the safety of his strong arms folding around you....

Feel his love....You are alone with Jesus in your favorite place.

I am going to give you a few moments to be alone with Jesus....Speak to him quietly in your heart....Ask him anything you want....Talk to him....Tell him all the things that are bothering you....*(Pause for half a minute or until children grow restless.)* Look up at Jesus, telling him, "Here I am, Lord. I am listening".... Now, listen to him speak....As you listen, feel the warmth of the sun on your face....*(Pause for half a minute or until children grow restless.)*

Prayer

Jesus, thank you for coming to my special place. I love you. I will come back to visit you often. Amen.

It is time for you to leave....Jesus wraps his arms around you and gives you a warm hug...."Goodbye for now," he says....Turn and walk away....Wave goodbye to Jesus.... Open your eyes and return to this room.

Part I

Advent
&
Christmas

Getting Ready for Jesus

Scripture: Mt 3:1-12; Mk 13:33-37
Feast: First Sunday of Advent (AB)
Music Suggestion: "When You Seek Me"/Gentle Sounds

As Christmas grows closer, there is a great deal of excitement in your home. Do your grandparents, aunts, uncles, or friends come to your house during this happy time? What are some things you are asked to do to prepare for this visit? (*Give the children time to respond.*) That's right! We are asked to clean up our rooms and throw away all the junk and broken toys in order to make our house ready for guests. Well, God sent a man called John the Baptist to prepare the way for Jesus' coming. John the Baptist begged the people to get ready for Jesus' coming by preparing their hearts to receive Jesus. John told the people to look into their hearts and to sweep away all those things that would not make Jesus feel welcome. This is a time for us to prepare our hearts for Jesus. Let us unzip our imaginations now to visit with Jesus in the desert near Jerusalem. Perhaps we will be able to see John the Baptist on our journey.

Meditation

Close your eyes....Take a deep breath....It is very, very quiet ....You feel the warm summer sun on your face....You are walking down a crooked path, up and down and around....

11

Rocks cut into your sandals....Sand from the desert land
sweeps over your feet as you walk....You are tired now and
want the journey to be over....At long last you see a group of
trees near the river....The limbs of the trees move with the
gentle summer breeze....Inviting you to enjoy their shade....
You move more quickly now to stand beneath the protecting
arms of the trees....The wind softly pulls at your hair....You
settle down onto the warm sand....Leaning against the bent
olive tree....Nearby you hear the waters of the Jordan River
splashing against the shore....A large crowd is gathered at the
riverside....Near the water's edge you see this man called John
the Baptist....He is dressed in the skins of animals....He stands
at the water's edge, urging people to join him....His voice is
firm as he speaks....His voice is carried on the wind....
"Prepare the way for the coming of God!"....You close your
eyes to rest, thinking...."What am I to do?....How can a child
such as me prepare for the coming of God?"....John, standing
ragged, a thick leather belt around his waist, motions wildly
with his arms....You study this man called John the Baptist....
What does he want with you?....He is looking directly at
you....There is a gentle touch on your shoulder....Jesus has
joined you in the shade of the old olive tree....He smiles at you
and calls you by name....The touch of Jesus' hand on your
shoulder makes you feel very special, doesn't it?....Jesus' face
grows serious...."I would like you to meet John the Baptist....
My Father has sent John the Baptist to prepare the people's
hearts for my coming. Listen to John"....You walk slowly
down the hillside toward John....Jesus remains in the shade of
the tree....He is smiling at you, encouraging you to join
John....John walks over to where you are standing....Kneeling
on one knee, John welcomes you. "There is much you can do
to prepare for the coming of God....Look into your heart.
Sweep away all those things that would not make Jesus feel
welcome"....Slowly make your way to where Jesus stands....

The people ask excitedly, "John, what should we do to
prepare for the promised one?"....John cups the cool
waters in his hand, splashing it upon his face, saying, "If

you really want to be good, you should share what you have with others, and be happy with the blessing God has given you"....Drawing closer, they ask John, "Who are you?" He is gentle now, kneeling on one knee, "I am simply a man who is telling all of you that the person God promised to send to save us is coming very soon. We should get ready by leading good lives. Be ready when he comes so you won't miss him"....

"Are you the promised one?" the people ask John....John shakes his head, pointing to the olive tree where you are standing with Jesus....Jesus turns his attention to you, "These people have never heard of me....No one has been baptized....You are the only person who knows me....If God asks you to tell the people about me, what will you tell them?"....

I will leave you alone with Jesus to talk about this. Think about all the things you would tell the people....

It is time to leave Jesus now....Say goodbye to Jesus....Turn and wave....Walk away....Open your eyes and return to this room.

Prayer
Jesus, help me to draw closer to you during the days before Christmas. Remind me of the things I should sweep away to make room for your love. Amen.

Discussion
- If God asked you to tell the people about Jesus, what would you tell them?
- If you were the only one who knew Jesus, what would you tell your friends about him?

A Morning with Mary

Scripture: Mt 1:18-25; Lk 1:26-38
Feast: Fourth Sunday of Advent (AB)
Music Suggestion: "Hail, Mary: Gentle Woman"/*Gentle Sounds*

Someone very special was born on Christmas. Does anyone know who it was? Why do you think God chose Mary to be Jesus' mother? God chose Mary to be the mother of Jesus because God loved Mary very much. Mary trusted God with her whole heart. Mary is our model of faith. Whom did God send to talk to Mary about becoming the mother of Jesus?

We are going to be with Mary the morning God sent his messenger, Gabriel, to visit with her. The angel Gabriel has just awakened Mary from a sound sleep.

Meditation

Close your eyes....Take a deep breath....Feel the quiet all the way to your toes....It is very early morning....The sun has just peeked over the hills of Galilee....Birds are singing their song with the light of dawn....

You are curled up in your bed covered with a tattered quilt ....Mary lies still in her bed....Slowly and quietly you turn in your covers....You look over at Mary....Her long dark hair covers the pillow....Mary is your friend....You feel warm all over when you think of your friendship....Mary suddenly sits

14

upright, startled out of her deep sleep....You are aware of a
bright light in the room....An angel stands at the foot of
Mary's wooden bed!...."Could this be Mary's guardian
angel?" you ask yourself....Mary grasps her ragged blanket
about her motioning for you to sit beside her....You feel her
tremble beneath the covers....The angel speaks, "Good
morning, Mary," slowly turning to greet you....The angel
calls you by name...."Do not be afraid, I have not come to
harm you"....Can you hear the angel's voice?....Mary places
her arms about you and smiles at the angel....You tremble
and shake all the way to your toes....

The angel is surely sent from God...."My name is Gabriel,"
the angel says gently....Gabriel turns now to speak to
Mary....Listen as the angel speaks...."Do not be afraid.
Mary, God has sent me to tell you that a male child is about
to be born....When the child is born he is to be named
Jesus....God wants to know if you are willing to be this
child's mother," Gabriel adds....Mary nods her head "yes"
but she looks at the angel and asks, "How can this be? I am
not married yet"....Mary's dark eyes are wide open....The
bright light surrounding the angel glows in her eyes....
Gabriel reaches down and touches Mary's dark curls...."God
wants you to have this baby, and he will perform a miracle
....Your child will be called the Son of God....But if you are
not willing to do this"....The angel's words are frozen in
mid-air....Mary scoots to the edge of her bed, falling to her
knees in prayer....The lovely young woman reaches out her
hand for you to kneel beside her....You feel the cold, hard
floor beneath your legs but Mary's hands are warm....Mary
speaks, "Whatever God asks of me, I will do....I do not
understand but I will trust in God....I will be the mother of
this child"....

The angel smiles warmly at Mary and disappears as quickly
as he appeared....Mary takes your hand in hers....She rises
to sit up on the bed....You are beside her on the bed....
Mary wraps your cold legs in the well-worn blanket....You

look up into her eyes, ready to speak....Mary knows what you are about to ask and answers...."We must put our whole trust in God at times"....

Take this time to speak to Mary....Ask her anything you want....Remember she always hears your prayers....Ask Mary to help you to trust in God. (*Pause for approximately half a minute or until the children are restless.*)

It is time to leave Mary....Feel her arms wrap around you, holding you close....Say goodbye....Turn and leave the room....Open your eyes and return to this room.

Prayer
Dearest Mary, thank you for saying "Yes" to God. Help me to know your son, Jesus. I love you. Amen.

Discussion
- How did Mary show that she trusted God?
- Do you think that Mary was surprised?
- Will Joseph be surprised?
- What are some ways that you show your trust in God?
- How can we prepare for Jesus' birthday?

Welcome, Mary!

Scripture: Lk 1:39-45
Feast: Fourth Sunday of Advent (C)
Suggested Music: "Hail, Mary: Gentle Woman"/*Gentle Sounds*

Whom do you like to visit most during the Christmas holidays? Why? Whom do you call first when you have special news to share? When you are in trouble? One day Mary was given some special news to share. Does anyone know what the special news was? That's right; the angel Gabriel told Mary that she was going to become the mother of Jesus. The angel also told her that her cousin Elizabeth was going to have a baby. Let's unzip our imaginations and join Mary in her tiny little room. The angel Gabriel has just vanished.

Meditation

Close your eyes....Wiggle your toes....Take a deep breath ....Let it out slowly......Whisper "Jesus".... Relax....

Mary's bedroom grows dark....Look at the place where the angel stood....A faint glow hangs in the air....Mary sits huddled on the edge of the bed....Look into her eyes.... They are as bright as the night star....Mary wraps her arm around your shoulders...."I must go to visit my cousin Elizabeth. The angel told me that she was going to have a child also....Dress quickly so that we may be on our way"....

Grab your shoes from under the bed....Your coat from the
back of a chair....Run your fingers through your hair....Mary
stands at the door of the small house, beckoning for you to
hurry....

It is early morning....The sun is peeking over the rooftops
....Listen, the roosters are crowing their wake-up call,
"Cockle-doodle-do"....Mary, taking your hand in hers, walks
very quickly down the path....Mary speaks with excitement,
"I can hardly wait to see Elizabeth. I have so much to tell
her"....The ground is cold and hard beneath your feet....
Over the hills....Past the lake....Through a small village of
Judah....Past the olive gardens....Down a crooked path....
Mary breaks into a run as you draw near her cousin's house
....Hurry to catch up with Mary....

At the end of the path stands a small cottage made of clay
....Flowers bloom beneath the tiny windows....The front
door opens....It is Elizabeth!....She is much older than Mary
....Elizabeth throws down her broom and rushes out to meet
you and Mary...."Welcome, Mary!" she calls out....Mary
throws her arms around her cousin...."Elizabeth!" Mary
cries....Elizabeth places her hand on her tummy, her eyes
grow large....Mary whispers in your ear, "Elizabeth just felt
her baby move within her"....Mary takes your hand and
together with Elizabeth you dance in a circle of joy....

Elizabeth invites you and Mary into her small home....She
prepares warm tea and cakes for her visitors....Mary warms
herself by the fire, inviting you to join her....The fire
crackles and pops....Elizabeth sits in a rocking chair....She
looks at Mary, then speaks, "Of all the women on earth,
you are most blessed. And the baby in your womb is also
blessed. I am so honored because you, the mother of my
Lord, have come to visit me!"....Elizabeth gets out of her
chair and drops on her knees before Mary, "You are
blessed, Mary, because you believed in the promise that
God made to you"....Elizabeth turns toward you, smiling,

18

"Child, it is Mary's faith and trust in God that make her special. Always be her friend."

Elizabeth returns to the kitchen....You are alone with Mary in front of the glowing fireplace....Mary takes your hand and places it on her tummy....Feel the soft stirring of baby Jesus beneath Mary's cloak....It reminds you of the soft fluttering of butterfly wings....This is the infant Jesus!.... Your Lord, your shepherd....Mary touches the back of your head....I will leave you alone with Mary for a few minutes.... Talk to Mary, the mother of Jesus.

Prayer

Loving God, just as Mary accepted that she would become the mother of Jesus, may I too believe and trust in your son, Jesus. This Christmas may I have joy enough to share. Peace enough to calm and love enough to light the world. Amen.

It is time to leave Mary now....Tell Mary and Elizabeth goodbye....Turn and walk through the door....Open your eyes and return to this room.

Discussion

- Why do you think Mary wanted to visit Elizabeth?
- What did Elizabeth do when she saw Mary?
- Do the people you visit say nice things about you?
- Do they help you feel happy?
- What do you do to help them feel happy?

Prayer Time

Supplies: large candle, slips of paper, pencils, basket or covered gift box with slit in top

1. Hand out small slips of paper and pencils. Remind the children of how Elizabeth blessed Mary. Ask them to think of people they would like to bless and to write the name on paper.

2. Darken the room. Light a candle, explaining that Jesus was like a light coming into a dark place. Invite the children to come forward to place the name of the person they would like to bless in the basket or gift box.

   CHILD: For (*name someone*), we ask God's blessings.

   CHILDREN: Jesus, hear our prayer.

4 The Birth of Jesus

In the Still of the Night

Scripture: Lk 2:1-16
Feast: Christmas (ABC)
Music Suggestion: "When You Seek Me"/*Gentle Sounds*
OR "Some Children See Him"/*December*

In those days, Caesar Augustus, the ruler of Rome, passed a law that everyone in his country should be counted. All the people went to the town where they were born to sign their names and the names of all the people in their families in a large book. This meant that Joseph and Mary were to make the long trip from Nazareth to the City of David, called Bethlehem, so that they could sign the book. While they were there the time came for Mary to give birth to her first-born son. Let us use our imaginations to walk with Mary and Joseph in the joy of this holy season.

Meditation

Close your eyes....Become very still....Open your heart and your imagination....Travel to the days so long ago....Take a deep breath....Whisper "Jesus"....Feel the quiet cover you like a warm blanket....It is just before sunset....The day is about to be clouded with darkness....You have walked many miles today....You can see the flickering lights of Bethlehem ahead....Clip-Clop, Clip-Clop, the donkey's hooves beat a rhythm on the dusty trail....The air is cold and filled with the smoke of weary travelers' campfires....

Joseph, the carpenter, walks beside you, his dark hair falling to his shoulders...."The city is going to be very crowded. I hope there is a room for us," he says to his pregnant wife, Mary....Mary, seated on the back of an old grey donkey, smiles and pulls her cloak around her....Mary looks very tired, her body rocking back and forth with each step of the donkey....As you draw close to the city, Joseph hands you the reins of his donkey....He asks you to look after Mary....Joseph hurries ahead to find a place to stay for the evening....Lead the donkey carrying Mary through the gates of the city....There are more people than you have ever seen before....People are pushing and shoving.... Making it difficult for you to hang on to the reins....Mary shudders and lets out a sigh....

At last Joseph returns....Worry and sadness cover his face....Joseph is unable to find a place to stay....Mary leans down and speaks softly in Joseph's ear....You realize that it is time for the child to be born...."Look after Mary, my child," Joseph says as he hurries through the crowds.... "God be with you," you call after Joseph....Mary lets out a deep sigh and reaches out to touch your shoulder...."The child is coming soon!" Mary tells you....You speak a prayer to God....There must be shelter somewhere....

Joseph is turned away from every house and every door.... You leave Mary and Joseph's side, determined to help.... Knocking on the back door of an inn you beg the innkeeper to help find shelter for Mary and Joseph....The innkeeper reluctantly motions down the road where there is a cave....He tells you that frequently animals are kept inside out of the weather, but it is clean and dry....Run to share the news with Mary and Joseph....The three of you set out toward the cave, down the crowded roadway....You are barely able to push your way through the people, through the trees, until at last you see the cave....

Joseph gently lifts Mary down from the back of the donkey. Joseph speaks firmly, "Child, go ahead and make a bed for Mary in the fresh hay"....Quickly gather the dry hay into a pile....Then smooth it out with your hands....The cave smells of hay and animals....A small lamb nestles in the hay nearby....A cow moos from the darkness of the cave....Animals too have found shelter here from the cold night air....Joseph guides Mary to the makeshift bed you have prepared for her....

Leave Mary and Joseph alone now....It is time for you to rest and to wait, praying for God's protection....Lay back on the hay....Sheep gather near you....You begin to pray....You feel God's presence all about you....God is here!....In the still of the long night you hear a baby's soft cry....Joseph stands beside you...."The child is a boy. His name shall be Jesus," he tells you....Joseph leads you to Mary's resting place....

Mary smiles as you enter....The baby is resting in Mary's arms....Joseph strokes the child's head....You look at Jesus....He is so small, so perfect....A tear of joy falls down your cheek....God's goodness is everywhere....Kneel down to give thanks to God....Mary raises on one elbow and invites you to come closer....She holds out her newborn son for you to hold...."Would you like to hold Jesus?" she asks ....Settle down close to Mary as she places the sleeping child in your arms....You are nervous....You are filled with joy....Take a moment to feel the warmth of the child in your arms, to feel the miracle of birth....Share this holy night with Jesus, Mary and Joseph. (*Pause for half a minute or until the children grow restless.*)

Prayer

Jesus, thank you for inviting me to be with you on this special day. I will always hold you in my heart. Welcome to our world. Amen.

If you listen very closely, you can hear angels in heaven singing beautiful songs to God...."Glory to God in the highest and peace on earth to people of good will."

It is now early morning....Crowds have gathered outside the cave....Shepherds from the nearby fields are offering praise to God. The shepherds tell of an angel that appeared to them, bringing news of great joy, "In the City of Bethlehem, a Savior has been born for you. This Savior is Christ the Lord."

It is time to tell Jesus and his family goodbye....Kiss baby Jesus' dimpled hand....Turn and walk away....Open your eyes and return to this room.

Discussion

- What is the most important gift you can give to Jesus? (*Yourself*)
- How can we give the gift of Jesus to others?
- What is your favorite part of this Christmas story?

Following His Star

Scripture: Mt 2:1-12
Feast: Epiphany (ABC)
Music Suggestion: "Some Children See Him"/*December*
   OR "Canyon of the Moon"/*Another Star in the Sky*

In the days of old, people believed a new star appeared in the sky each time a child was born. One night some people spotted an extra bright star in the sky. They decided that someone important had been born, someone who would outshine everyone else. Remembering the scriptures of old, they felt that surely the Messiah had been born. They set out on their search, following the star.

Let's unzip our imaginations, joining the wise men in their search for the baby born in a simple stable, our Lord of Lords, Jesus.

Meditation

Close your eyes....Take a deep breath....Let it out slowly....Put everything else out of your mind....Relax....

You are near the gates of the city of Jerusalem....It is evening....Glowing lanterns light up the shops and houses ....People are scurrying about, gathering their belongings.... Watch the activity....Donkeys loaded with the city's treasures walk past you, through the gate....A small group of men approaches the city....They glance upward several times, pointing to the sky....A tall, dark-skinned man, dressed in a flowing red cloak, speaks to you, "Where is the newborn King of the Jews?"....Before you can answer, he stops a band of merchants...."Where is the King of the Jews?....We have seen his star in the east and have come to worship him"....You have heard rumors about the baby born in a stable....Go up to the travelers, offering to go with them on their journey...."Welcome, Child. But first we must eat. Will you watch our belongings?"....The men leave their donkeys and three wrapped packages with you....You settle down on your haunches, waiting....

A small group of King Herod's soldiers, their swords shining in the moonlight, question citizens, asking, murmuring, "Where is the Messiah? Where was he born?"....One soldier, his lantern swinging from side to side, runs off toward King Herod's castle....You shudder in the cold evening air....

The three wise men join you now, packing their belongings onto the backs of the mules....Suddenly, you hear a trumpet's sounding voice...."The King is coming! The King is coming!" shout the soldiers....King Herod steps from his horse....You have never seen the king this close....He is dressed in blue velvet....A crown of gold sits upon his head of black curls....He is a large man with a booming voice.... The ground seems to shake when he speaks....By now, many people have gathered around the king, including leaders of the Jewish people....."Where is this Messiah to be born?" the king growls....Wise men answer, "The sacred scriptures tell us that the Messiah will be born in Bethlehem."

The King walks back and forth, strutting his power.... Turning to the wise men he roars, "Tell me the exact time you first noticed the star"....The king now turns toward you, "Go and find out all you can about the child. When you have found him, come back and tell me so I may go also and worship him"....The wise men from the east think the King is being kind....But you know in your heart of hearts that the king really wants to kill the newborn child....

You slink back out of view, joining the three men from the east....As night settles, you and the wise men begin the journey across the desert sands....Your feet settle deep into the soft sand with each step....The night is covered in darkness, except for the brilliant light of the star....The star appears to travel just ahead of the journeyers....It shines brighter than any star that you have ever seen...."Surely this must be a sign," you think to yourself....Everyone is talking at once, pointing excitedly to the sky...."What will you bring the new king?" one voice calls out in the night air...."I have brought the gift of gold," calls another....The wise man dressed in a cape of fur looks your way, announcing, "I have brought a gift of rare perfume, one only the rich can afford"....Your hands quickly go through the pockets of your clothing....Surely you will find the baby king and have nothing to offer....

After many hours of travel in the stillness of the night, you reach Bethlehem....The star now shines more brilliantly than before....It lights your way through the cobblestone streets and rows of little houses....The only sound you hear are the Click-Clack of the donkey's hooves and the quiet shuffling of footsteps....Specks of light seep from the cracks around the doorway. At last the star appears to have stopped....The path of light from the star falls upon a small stable....The wise men whisper in the darkness...."This is where we will find the Messiah. Child, go now and knock on the door....Tell the child's parents that we have come to worship their newborn son, the promised Messiah"....You make your way to the doorway of the cave....Put your ear to the doorway....The soft sounds of an infant's cooing reach your ear....Knock on the makeshift door....Knock again....The man called Joseph comes to the door....He greets you warmly, offering his calloused hands....Tell

Joseph why you have come....Joseph peeks out the door, then waves an invitation for the three wise men to come in....

Joseph shows you into a dimly lit corner of the stable.... Mary sits upon a bed made of straw, wrapped in the warmth of a woven blanket....Nearby, the child, Jesus, lies in a makeshift cradle....Mary takes your hand, leading you to the babe....Look at this tiny child, his hand wrapped around your little finger....He is so small, so perfect....Your heart begins to pound more rapidly....This is the Lord. This is your Savior....Fall upon your knees, giving thanks to God for bringing you to this special place....You feel the warmth of love flow from your head to your feet....

The wise men kneel at the foot of the manger, giving their thanks to God....The gold shines in the light of a nearby lantern....The gifts of frankincense and myrrh lie yet unopened....Mary smiles at you, "His name is Jesus," she says warmly....You dig into your pockets once again.... Surely there must be something that you could give baby Jesus....

I am going to leave you for a moment with Mary and Joseph and Jesus....Speak to Jesus with your heart....Tell him what gift you are going to give him....Is it something you love to do? Something from home? Your talents and gifts? Your love?

Prayer
Dear sweet Jesus, thank you for being a part of my life. I love you. Welcome to my heart. Amen.

The sun is rising above the rooftops, replacing the cold dark of night with the warmth and light of day....The wise men have begun their journey back to their homelands....It is time for you to leave now....Say goodbye to Mary, Joseph, and the babe....Walk out the door of the house....Hear the roosters crow in the distance....Open your eyes and come back into this room....

Discussion

* The three wise men gave the best gift they could possibly give to the child Jesus. If Jesus were born today, what gift would you bring?

A Voice over the Water

Scripture: Mt 3:11-17; Mk 1:7-11; Lk 3:15-16,21-22
Feast: Baptism of the Lord (ABC)
Music Suggestion: "Sea of Change"/*Ceremony*
      OR **"By Name I Have Called You"/*Gentle Sounds***

Does anyone remember going to a baptism? Today we are going to use our imaginations to travel to the day Jesus was baptized in the Jordan River. Jesus, hearing that John the Baptist was preaching near the Jordan River, decided to go and listen to John talk. At the end of his talk, John asked people to walk into the river and be baptized to show that they wanted to lead good lives. Jesus walked into the water. John was really surprised! Unzip your imagination now as you join Jesus near the shores of the Jordan River.

Meditation

Optional: Play a tape of the sounds of the sea or rain falling. Ask the children to imagine the sounds of water and the life it gives.

Close your eyes....Draw a deep breath....Let it out slowly.... Your arms and legs feel very relaxed....Imagine the sounds of water and the life it gives....You are sitting on a green hillside ....Lambs play nearby....Watch them tumbling in the tall grass....Birds fly about you, red birds, blue birds, and tiny little sparrows....Listen to them singing their song to the

30

Lord....Feel the warm sun on your back....This is going to be a good day!....

You look far below....The blue-green waters of the Jordan River wash against the sandy shore....The valley is brown and barren except for a few small trees....You do not want to leave this happy spot high above the valley....But, sadly, it is time to make your way down the hill....

Walk slowly down the path....Your feet slip and slide on the loose rocks....You hear footsteps not far behind...."May I walk with you?" a gentle voice calls out....Turning, you see it is your friend Jesus!....Jesus calls your name, smiling warmly...."Come, let me hold your hand so you don't slip on the path"....Take Jesus' hand....It is much larger than yours....His skin is tanned from the desert sun....It is good to see your friend again....Hold his hand tightly.

You are nearly at the bottom of the hillside when Jesus points to a large crowd gathered on the shore...."All of those people have come to be baptized by my cousin John" ....Jesus walks faster now....You are almost running to keep up with him....Clouds of sand cover your feet as you walk ...."There is John. He is standing in the river near the shore," Jesus says excitedly....John is wearing an animal skin....A rope belt is pulled tightly about his waist....His hair is long and uncombed....People are wading out into the river waters....John is bent over now, his hands cupped, dipping into the water....A child about your age stands in front of John....John pours the refreshing water over the child's head....The child is happy and smiling....You wonder about this....Jesus, knowing your question, answers, "These people are asking John to baptize them show that they want to lead good lives and that they will be ready for my coming"....

"Walk with me, my child. I want John to baptize me," Jesus motions for you to follow...."We will ask John to baptize you,

also, and then myself"....Still holding Jesus' hand, walk into
the water....Feel the rocky shore beneath your feet....Small
waves of water splash against your legs, Almost pulling you
further out into the water....John looks into your eyes,
smiles, and calls you by name....He places his strong, rough
hand on your shoulder...."I am baptizing you in water, but
someone is coming who is greater than I am....I am not
worthy of tying his sandals....He will baptize you with the
Holy Spirit".....John dips his hands into the water, then
slowly pours the cool water over your head....Feel the water
trickle down your face....Lick your lips....Taste the water....
A warm feeling fills you from head to toe....Jump up and
down in the life-giving water....Jesus smiles, then takes his
place before John....

Jesus, standing, bows his head....A tear forms on John's
cheek, perhaps a tear of joy....John looks startled, "Jesus,
you should baptize me"....Jesus shakes his head "no," then
speaks in a whisper to John....Jesus raises his hands in
prayer as John begins to pour the water over Jesus' head....

As Jesus stands praying, his cloak heavy with water, the
clouds separate....A beautiful dove flies above Jesus' head
....Listen carefully....In the quiet of the moment you hear
the gentle brush of angels' wings signaling the voice of
God....A voice from above announces, "This is my Son. I
love him very much".....The people gasp in awe, falling on
their knees....

Jesus turns, takes your hand, and leads you to the shore....
Walk the short distance around the water's edge....Jesus stops
near a pile of driftwood....He speaks quietly, "God has called
you by name....The Holy Spirit of God rests within your
heart"....Feel your heart pounding...."You will have the
strength and joy to do good things for God in the world"....
Jesus settles on a rock, warming himself in the last rays of the
sun...."Remember, my child, that God has picked you out and
called you by name so that you can go to work for him"....

"But I am just a child....What can I do for God?" you ask....
The Lord smiles....He lifts you into his arms...."I will show
you the way....Will you follow me?"

Take this time to be with Jesus....(*Pause for half a minute
or until the children are restless.*)

Prayer
*Jesus, show me the way to God's kingdom. I will
follow you. Send your Holy Spirit so that I might be a
messenger of your Good News. Amen.*

It is time to leave....Give Jesus a hug....Feel his strong arms
around you....Tell Jesus goodbye for now....Open your eyes
and return to this room....

Discussion

- How does it feel to know that God picked you to work
  for the kingdom of God?
- How can you follow Jesus this week?

Prayer Service

*You may prefer to use this prayer service rather than
discussion time.*

1. Gather the children in a circle. Dim the lights, lighting
   one large candle in the center of the room. On the table
   place two large bowls of water, a white garment, and a
   baptismal candle. Explain to the children that candles
   remind us that God calls us to live the light of Jesus.

   LEADER: We are brothers and sisters in God's
   family. Let us renew the promise of our
   baptism to live as Jesus did, always trying to do
   what God wants.

33

LEADER: Do you believe God, our creator, wants us to be happy?

ALL: I do! alleluia!

LEADER: Do you believe in Jesus?

ALL: I do! Alleluia!

LEADER: Do you believe in the Holy Spirit, who lives in us to help us follow Jesus?

ALL: I do! Alleluia!

LEADER: Do you believe that after we die we will rise again with Jesus to live with God forever?

ALL: I do! Alleluia!

LEADER: God is calling each of you by name.
Help us to follow him faithfully. Amen.

2. Invite children to dip both hands in water, first with fists clenched, demonstrating how hard it is to always live as Christians, then slowly open hands, inviting the Spirit of God to work through them, sign themselves and repeat:

I belong to God's family. God loves me.

Part II

Lent
&
Easter

Jesus Shines As Brightly As the Sun

Scripture: Mk 9:2-10; Lk 9:28-36a
Feast: Second Sunday of Lent (ABC)
Music Suggestion: "Eye Has Not Seen"/*Instruments of Peace*

Does anyone remember seeing previews of coming attractions when you go to the movies? What movies are you looking forward to seeing? It is fun to see what is coming up, isn't it? One day Jesus gave a few of his friends a preview of what he would be like after the resurrection.

Jesus and his disciples spent six days speaking to people in villages around Philippi. They were very tired of travel and the crowds. The disciples were surprised when Jesus invited his friends, Peter, James, and John to join him in climbing to a high mountaintop. Let's unzip our imaginations, joining Jesus and his friends in what turned out to be an amazing journey.

Meditation

Close your eyes....Wiggle your toes one last time....Take a deep breath in....Now let your breath out....Whisper "Jesus"....Relax....

You are climbing a very steep hill....You have been climbing
for hours....Butterflies flit from one wild flower to another,
fluttering their colorful wings of red, purple and blue....
Ground squirrels scamper across the mountain trail....Jesus
turns and motions for you to hurry and join his side....
James sits down upon a weathered tree stump, trying to
catch his breath....Peter, the oldest, pushes past you to
speak with Jesus....Listen to Peter's puffing and panting....
Jesus calls back to you, "Did you ever see a more beautiful
day?"....You are so tired that your legs feel heavy, like a
block has been tied to each foot...."Please, Jesus, can we
stop for awhile?" you ask....Jesus turns, smiling, "We will
soon be at the top. Look around you....All of this beauty is
my Father's gift to you. Don't waste time complaining.
Enjoy the beauty that God has given to you"....Look down
into the valley far below....Lambs graze on the sloping
hillside....But, the top of the mountain seems so far away....

At long last, you arrive at the mountain's crest....It is almost
flat....Large boulders of rocks burst free of the mountain's
grasp, casting long shadows in the moonlight. The wind is
blowing your hair, blushing your cheeks with its cool
breath....Jesus drops to his knees and begins to pray....
Looking over his shoulder, Jesus speaks to you and the
disciples, "Join me now in prayer, giving thanks to God for
our many blessings"....Peter murmurs, "It's about time we
rest," as he drops to the ground, folding his legs beneath
him. Peter lowers his head, touching the ground with his
forehead in prayer, according to the custom of the day....
Soon, all fall asleep except you and Jesus....

Use this time to think of all the wonderful gifts that God has
given you....A family....A home....Friends....Think of all the
goodness God has provided you....Give thanks to God for
these gifts....(*Pause briefly.*)....Peter's grumbling has
stopped and you see a smile on his weather-beaten face as
he falls into deep slumber....Put your head down now in
prayer.

Feel the presence of a warm glow....Look up....It is the
brightest light that you have ever seen....Cup your hands
over your eyes....The light is brighter than the sun!....Jesus
remains kneeling, glowing in the light....His clothes become
as white as the as new snow, whiter than anyone could
bleach them....Rub your eyes....Jesus is talking to two old
men...."How did they get up to the mountaintop?" you ask
yourself. Peter has come to his feet, his mouth wide open at
the wonder of what he sees before him....He cries out, "It is
Moses and Elijah; they have returned from the dead!"

Jesus is speaking to Elijah, the prophet of Jesus' coming,
and God's favored leader, Moses....Strain to hear what they
are saying....The three men of God are discussing how
Jesus is going to die in Jerusalem....Can you hear them?....
You shudder, knowing these words are not for your ears....
Peter interrupts, "Teacher, lucky that we are all here with
you, we will begin to build three shelters, one for you, one
for Moses, and one for Elijah"....Your heart is pounding
with fear....What is happening?....Peter's mouth moves a
mile a minute, talking on and on about buildings....James
covers his eyes, shielding them from the light....James
whispers in your ear, "Peter is frightened too; he just
doesn't know what else to do or say so he keeps on talking."

In an instant the shadow of a cloud appears and covers
everyone with its soft, billowing arms....You cannot see
above you or below....There is just the cloud....Even Peter is
quiet now....A deep voice comes from the cloud, "This is
my Son, whom I love. Listen to him"....Surely this must be
the voice of God!....The cloud lifts from the mountaintop....
Only Jesus remains....You and James, John and Peter
huddle together, talking of what you have seen this day.

It is now nearly dark as the four of you and Jesus make your
way down the mountainside....Loose rocks cause you to
stumble....Darkness is closing in....Jesus stops and turns to
you, offering his hand....Look up into Jesus' eyes,

questioning what you have seen....He winks and places his finger across his lips...."Shhh!"....

Jesus stops by a clump of trees to rest. Drawing you close to him, he says, "Sometimes people feel God very close to them when they are out in the woods.... Others feel God is near when they are helping others or praying"....Jesus looks deep within your eyes and asks, "When do you feel close to God?" I will leave you alone with Jesus to talk about this. Look into your heart and speak to Jesus. (*Pause for half a minute or until they are restless.*)

Prayer

Jesus, when you were on the mountaintop you became bright with light, like a star glowing in the night. Help me to be filled with your light and your love. Amen.

You are at the bottom of the mountain now....It is time for you to leave....Say goodbye to Jesus and his friends.... Always remember this time with Jesus....Open your eyes and return to this room.

Discussion

- What happened while you were on the mountaintop with Jesus?
- What did God say to James, John, and Peter about Jesus?
- How do we listen to Jesus today? Have you ever felt close to God? Where were you?

Living Waters

Scripture: Jn 4:5-15,19-30
Feast: Third Sunday of Lent (A)
Music Suggestion: "Song over the Water"/*Instruments of Peace*

Have you ever eaten a bowl of salty popcorn? What do you want when you have finished? Have you ever played a fast game on a hot day? What do you want to help you cool off?

One day Jesus was walking near a village in Samaria when he became very thirsty and tired. He sat down by Jacob's Well to rest for a while, but he didn't have anything to dip the water from the well. While Jesus was by the well he talked with a woman about "living waters." Let's unzip our imaginations to join Jesus at Jacob's Well to taste of the living waters.

Meditation

Close your eyes....Wiggle your toes....Take a deep breath ....Let it out slowly....Whisper "Jesus"....Relax....

It is a hot summer day....You and your friends are playing in the town square....A large ball made of goatskin is the target....Kick the ball....Sending it flying through the air....Run....Jump....Toss the ball....Dirt clouds the air as you rough and tumble across the courtyard....Perspiration pours down your face....Water—you must have a drink of

41

water....Make your way toward the village well....All you can think about is a cool, refreshing drink of water....

Quickly skip down the winding path to the well....You can almost taste the water....There is a man sitting on the side of the well....It is Jesus!....He looks very tired and very hot ....You are so happy to see Jesus you almost forget about getting a drink from the well....He looks toward you and smiles...."There is no dipper for the water. Come and wait with me; someone will come along soon and give us a drink"....Jesus points toward the ball you are carrying...."I had a ball like that when I was a boy," Jesus recollects fondly....Jesus takes the ball from your hand....Your eyes meet....For a minute it is as though he can look deep inside you....Jesus passes the ball back to you, kicking up a cloud of dust with his sandaled feet....

You grow tired of sitting in the hot sun....Your mouth is as dry as a mouthful of cotton balls....Jesus places his hand on your shoulder...."Relax....There is no need to look for a dipper. Someone is coming this way soon"....You wonder how Jesus could know what is on your mind....

At long last, when you are about to give up on ever getting a drink of water, a women from the village appears at the well.

Jesus speaks to the woman, "Would you be so kind to give us a drink from the well?"....The young dark-haired woman looks surprised...."You are a Jew. Why do you ask me, a Samaritan woman, for a drink?"....The woman is surprised because Jews were not supposed to speak to Samaritans.... She glances toward you, then speaks again to Jesus, "No one like you has ever asked me for anything." Jesus startles her by answering, "If you knew who I was, you would ask me to give you living water so you would never thirst again"...."Living water?" the woman mutters, lowering her bucket into the well...."Does the child want a drink also?"

she says, looking your direction....Shake your head "yes" quickly. Jesus stands now, adjusting the rope belted around his waist, "Anyone who drinks from this well will be thirsty again, but whoever drinks from the water I give them will never be thirsty again"....

The woman slowly fills a cup from her wooden bucket.... Carefully studying Jesus, she says, "You sound like you are pretty important. Who are you? Are you a prophet?" Jesus shakes his head slightly, brushing his hair aside....A summer wind sends twisting coils of sandy earth twirling across the courtyard....Jesus sips the cool water, then, handing the cup to you, he smiles and gestures for you and the woman to sit down with him....Jesus begins to tell the woman things about herself which only she and God would have known....Her eyes are wide with amazement...."I do believe you are truly a holy person!" The woman falls to her knees before Jesus, "I know that the Messiah—that is, Christ—is coming soon," she tells Jesus. Jesus looks at you and smiles, then, leaning against the well, he replies, "I am he, the one who is speaking to you"....The woman cries in joy, "You are my Lord!"....The woman grasps your hands, pulling you to your feet....Joining hands, your arms encircle Jesus....Dance and circle Jesus with love and happiness.

You and the woman now sit beside Jesus in the shade of the well....Curl your legs under you....Listen to Jesus explain what he meant by "living waters"...."If the living waters work through you, you will grow to understand that it should not matter what color a person's skin is or where he comes from....God wants you to always do good for others and love all of God's children."

The sun is beginning to set....Long shadows criss-cross the courtyard....Jesus stands, "It is time for you both to return home"....The woman gathers her water jug. Jesus gives her a hug, then waves as she disappears down the road...."She will lead many others to believe in me and the importance of living a good life." Jesus places his hands on your shoulders and, calling you by name, he asks, "Will you lead others to believe in me?" I will leave you for a moment so that you can speak to Jesus.

Prayer

Jesus, I believe in you even though I do not see you. May I lead others to you and spread the joy of your Good News. Amen.

Tell Jesus goodbye for now....Walk away....Turn and wave ....Open your eyes and return to this room.

Discussion

- Pretend you are a Samaritan. Would you believe this woman when she tells you about Jesus? Why?
- How would you tell someone about Jesus?

Allow the children to come forward and refresh themselves with a cool drink of water.

9 The Prodigal Son

A Boy Comes Home

Scripture: Lk 15:11-32
Feast: Fourth Sunday of Lent (C)
Music Suggestion: "Pardon Your People"/*Gentle Sounds*

Has anyone ever been lost or separated from your parents in a big store or perhaps when you were out camping? What did it feel like? How did you feel when you saw your parents again? How did your parents act? Relieved? Happy? One thing is for sure: they were worried about you because they love you. Do you think that God ever worries about you? When does God worry most about us?

When we do things that we know are wrong, this separates us from God. We are lost until we are able to say, "I'm sorry."

Jesus loved talking to people about God's love and forgiveness. He would talk to them in boats, in the fields, in towns, and in synagogues.

One day Jesus told a story about a kind and loving father and two sons. Jesus told the story to help us understand what God's forgiveness is like. Let's unzip our imaginations and listen to Jesus tell the story.

Meditation

Close your eyes....Take a deep breath....Let it out slowly....
Whisper "Jesus"....Relax....

You are sitting on the edge of an old wooden dock....
Dangle your feet in the cool water....If you are very quiet
you can hear the sea gulls....There is one over there to the
right!....The grey and white bird dives deep into the waves
....Here he comes....A small fish clasped tightly in his
beak....Swarms of tiny minnows swim in circles beneath the
dock....

The summer sun wraps the day in its warm rays....A group
of children play nearby....Laughter and happiness are
everywhere....Feel a tap on your shoulder....Turn around....
It's Jesus!....Jump up and give him a hug....Jesus invites
you to join the other children in the shade of an old gnarled
tree....Happily you skip along the path....Jesus lowers
himself to the grass....He pats the ground next to him,
motioning for you to sit beside him....Jesus smiles at all the
children....Then he begins his story.

There once was a father who had two sons. The younger
one said to his dad, "Father, out of what you have, give me
my share of the property." So the father divided what he
had between his two sons. Not many days later, the
younger son sold his property and left home with the
money. The father was very sad. He would miss his son. He
loved him very much. The younger son did lots of foolish
things because he had no one to guide him. He bought a
fancy house and a big long car. Every night he threw a big
party, inviting people he didn't even know. He wanted to
have fun all the time. One day he went to his money bag
and found that all the money was gone.

He had no place to stay and he had no money to buy food.
All his so-called friends left him. So he went to work for a

46

man who had pigs. He was hungry enough to eat what the pigs ate. He was very unhappy. He began to think of home and said to himself, "The servants in my father's house have plenty of food. Yet here I am dying of hunger. I will go back to my father and say, "I've done many wrong things and I don't deserve to be your son any more. But would you let me work for you as one of the hired servants?"

Every day since his son had left for the city, the father watched for his return. The father would stand on the hillside, peering into the distance. While he was still far off, his father saw the son. The son fell on his knees, saying, "I've done many wrong things and I am sorry." The father was so happy that his son had "turned around" and come home again, he ran to meet him crying out, "We'll have a party and celebrate." But the older son was jealous. He didn't think that the father should be so willing to forgive his brother's mistakes. He decided not to go to the party. The father went to his older son and told him that he understood why he felt the way he did but he should be happy that the younger boy had returned and was sorry for all the things he did wrong...."That's why we are going to have a party," he added.

Jesus takes your hand....Jesus places his arm around your shoulder...."God loves you just like the father in that story. Even when you make mistakes and do things that you shouldn't, God is always waiting to forgive and welcome you with waiting arms. God loves you this much," Jesus stretches his long arms out, showing you how much God loves you....Jesus holds you close to his side, whispering, "Do you ever find it hard to say 'I'm sorry?' (Pause.) Is it hard to forgive someone who hurts you? How can I help you?"

I will leave you alone for a while so you can talk to Jesus. Tell him what is on your heart.

Prayer

Jesus, thank you for reminding me of God's constant love, of God's forgiveness of my mistakes even when I really mess up. Help me to be a loving, forgiving friend. Amen.

It is time to leave now....Tell Jesus goodbye....Turn and walk down the grassy knoll....Wave goodbye....Open your eyes and return to this room.

Discussion

- Why did the younger son decide to go back home?
- What was his father doing?
- What did he do when he saw his son?
- How do you think the son felt?
- Why do you think the older brother felt as he did?
- Do any of you know the special sacrament that we have to celebrate God's forgiveness?

Jesus' Friend Dies

Scripture: Jn 11:1-45
Feast: Fifth Sunday of Lent (B)
Music Suggestion: "We Believe in You"/*Gentle Sounds*

Have you ever lost something that was very special to you?
Has a pet or person you loved died? (*Remind the children
that if we believe in Jesus, we will have life everlasting.*)
It is very sad to lose someone or something you love, isn't
it? Do you think that Jesus ever cried? Well, one day Jesus
did cry. One of his special friends, Lazarus, died and Jesus
was very sad. Let's unzip our imaginations, joining Jesus on
the other side of the Jordan River, in the land where John
the Baptist once preached.

Meditation

Close your eyes....Wiggle your toes....Take a deep breath
....Let it out slowly....Whisper "Jesus".... Relax....

You are sitting on a hillside, waiting for your friend Jesus....
The sun warms the back of your neck....A tiny
hummingbird flits from flower to flower, his long beak
reaching deep within the blossoms....Children play with a
ball made of goatskin....It rolls to you....Kick the ball back to
the waiting children....Jesus is surrounded by people....
People stretch to touch even the hem of his clothing....A
man bursts through the crowd, carrying a rolled piece of

49

paper....You take the scroll from the old messenger....It is a message for Jesus from his friends Martha and Mary of Bethany....Hand the rolled message to Jesus....Jesus reads out loud to you, "Dear Jesus, Our brother Lazarus is very sick. We think he is going to die. Please come quickly. Love Martha and Mary"....

Jesus sees you are worried about Lazarus. He whispers, "Lazarus will not die, my child"....For two more days you stay by Jesus' side as he tells the people about the kingdom of God....Finally, he announces, "It is time now that we make our way to the home of Lazarus....He has fallen asleep and I am going to wake him up"....Taking Jesus' hand, you and the disciples set out for Bethany....A herd of goats crosses the path....Jesus reaches out and pats a little black billy goat on the head....As the dust settles on the road you see a woman running toward you....She is waving her arms....It is Martha....Pulling her veil over her face she calls out, "Lazarus is dead! He has been in his tomb for four days! If you had been here maybe my brother would still be alive"....Jesus takes Martha into his loving arms...."Don't worry. Your brother will come to life again. I am the source of all life," he tells her....

"But, Jesus," you interrupt...."Trust me, my child," he states....

Many people have gathered at Lazarus' tomb....Mary, his sister, runs to Jesus' side...."Why didn't you come right away?" she cries....Mary buries her head in her hands and cries in sadness....Your eyes fill with tears....Sadness fills the air....Jesus lowers his head in sorrow....Tears fall freely down his cheeks....Jesus moves to the shade of a nearby tree....Leaning on its huge trunk, he sobs....Reaching out for the comfort of your love, Jesus takes your hand in his.... Feel this sorrow....Wipe away the tears from Jesus' eyes.... Opening your hand, you see a tear drop glistening in the sunlight....

Jesus walks over to Martha and Mary...."I know what is in your heart....Show me where you have laid him"....Tag along behind Jesus to the tomb of Lazarus....A huge rock covers the entrance to the tomb....Jesus commands his disciples, "Take away the stone"....Martha speaks, "Oh, no, Lord, there will be a bad odor. He has been there for four days." You help the disciples roll the heavy stone away.... Jesus looks toward the heavens, raising his arms in prayer to his Father, then, moving closer to the doorway of the tomb, he commands, "Lazarus, come out!"....Everyone stands in silence, watching Jesus....Once more he calls out, "Lazarus, come out here!"....At long last you here a sound from within the tomb, a stirring....A few moments later, Lazarus walks from the tomb, his burial clothing falling from his shoulders....Mary and Martha embrace their brother.... All the people gather around Lazarus, weeping in joy.... Lazarus is alive!....The air rings with happiness and joy.

Jesus once again takes your hand and leads you to the shade of the olive tree...."Do you understand that Lazarus died so that my friends would grow to believe in the glory of God? I love you as much as I love Lazarus, and I wish to give you new life here on earth and everlasting life in heaven. New life comes from knowing me. Mary and Martha wished only that their brother would live....I granted that wish. If you could have one wish come true, what would you wish for?"....Jesus waits for your answer....

I will leave you alone for a few moments to talk to Jesus.

Prayer
Dear Jesus, thank you for being my friend. Thank you for my special friends and family, who brought me to your side. Help me to always trust and believe in you. Amen.

It is time to leave Jesus now....Give him a hug....Feel his arms around you....Walk away from the olive tree....Turn and wave....Come back into this room.

Discussion

- How would you feel if your best friend did not come when you needed him/her? Do you think this is how Martha and Mary felt?
- Why do you think that Jesus waited so long before setting out to see Lazarus? Do you think that God had something else in mind?
- Jesus did not cry when told of Lazarus' death, but he did cry when he went to the tomb. Why? How did you feel when you saw Jesus crying?

Activity: Wishing Game

Ask the children to offer suggestions about how to end this phrase, "If I could have one wish come true, I'd wish...."

- If Martha, Mary, and Lazarus were to play the Wishing Game, what might be their wishes? Why?

Hail to the King!

Scripture: Lk 22:14-23,56
Feast: Palm/Passion Sunday (ABC)
Music Suggestion: "Gather Us In"/*Instruments of Peace*

Do you like to go to a parade? What is your favorite parade
to watch? Why do we have parades? Parades are often in
celebration of a season or in honor of an event, such as
Fourth of July parades. Many times parades are to honor a
special person. One day Jesus was in a parade. The people
of Jerusalem greeted him with a parade of honor. But
within a few days he was put to death on the cross. Do you
ever wonder what you would have done or what you would
have said to Jesus during those last days? Let's unzip our
imaginations to join the cheering crowd.

Meditation

Close your eyes....Take a deep breath....Wiggle your toes
one more time....Relax. It is early evening....You are
standing by the side of a well-traveled road....Clouds of dust
rise from the road with each step you take....More people
than you have ever seen pass by you: old ladies, little
children, all going to celebrate Passover....You look up into
their faces....They look very tired but the air is filled with
excitement and laughter....Can you see all the people?....
Dust blows across the roadway....

The voices grow louder now....The throngs of people move to either side of the roadway....There is excitement in the air....You can feel it....The same feeling you have waiting for your birthday or when something wonderful is about to happen....People are murmuring, pushing and shoving to be in front of the crowd....The voices are louder now, almost shouting, "He's coming!"

Jesus is coming!....You push your way through the crowd and climb into the branches of a tree....Look up the road.... Do you see Jesus?....He is riding on the back of a donkey; his red cloak hangs about his shoulders....People are shouting now....Some are laying palm leaves on the roadway....One man removes his coat and places it in the middle of the road....You wonder about this....

You quickly climb down from the gnarled old branches of the tree, pushing your way through the people....Someone almost steps on you....You are on the road at last....You see Jesus and his friends....One man is leading the donkey ....You hear Jesus call his name, "John"....As you make your way toward Jesus, you pass by several groups of men ....They are speaking about Jesus....Their words are harsh ....You hear them speak of death....Suddenly you feel frightened for Jesus....You must warn him....You break into a run....Your feet are almost flying down the path....You are running to meet Jesus.

You are now standing in front of Jesus....You feel the warmth of the donkey's breath....John helps Jesus down from the donkey's back....You are almost close enough to reach out and touch him....You stretch as far as you can.... You touch his cloak....Can you feel the roughness of the cloth?....Jesus turns around....He is looking right at you.... He is smiling....He speaks your name....Can you hear him? ....The crowds are rushing in to get a glimpse of Jesus.... Two of Jesus' disciples begin to lift him to the back of a colt

....You pull off your own coat and throw it on the donkey's back to soften the ride of Jesus....

Jesus begins his ride into Jerusalem....People are cheering ....Jesus smiles and waves....You must tell Jesus of the danger you fear....As a sign of honor and respect, the people begin to spread their coats along the road before him....Others throw palm branches onto the dirty roadway ....The disciple called Peter hands you the reins of the donkey....You are leading the colt....Jesus smiles at you.... You are a part of this joyous parade....The crowd begins to cheer...."Hail to the king!"....Can you hear the crowds?....

Jesus signals for the parade to stop, taking your hand....He lifts you onto the donkey's back....You feel the safety of Jesus' arms around you....You are riding with Jesus through the streets of Jerusalem....Clip-Clop ring the donkey's hooves....The people are waving and cheering....Jesus seems to not notice the crowd....He lowers his head and speaks only to you....Listen to his words of love....Jesus asks you, "What can I do for you, my child?"....Speak to Jesus with your heart....Welcome Jesus into your life.... (*Pause for half a minute.*)

Prayer

Jesus, I love you. Thank you for living and dying for me. Thank you for rising to new life. I will always be your friend. Amen.

It is time to leave....It might be hard to say goodbye, but Jesus understands....Tell Jesus that you love him....Turn and walk away through the crowd....Open your eyes and return to this room.

Discussion

- How did you feel during the parade? Happy? Excited? Why?

- Jesus rode into Jerusalem like a king. Everyone knew that Jesus was a king. But Jesus was a different kind of king. He was a wise and wonderful king. What kingdom does Jesus rule? (*Heaven and earth*)

- Do your know what happens next Sunday? (*Explain that Holy Week does not end with the death of Jesus but with Easter Sunday, which is the following Sunday.*)

- If you had been in Jerusalem with Jesus, do you think that you could have changed what happened?

Do This in Memory of Me

Scripture: Mt 26:26-29; Mk 14:22-25; Lk 22:17-20
Feast: Days of Lent (ABC)
Music Suggestion: "I Will Never Forget You"/Gentle Sounds

How do you remember someone who is very important to you? Some people carry pictures in their wallets or hang pictures in their houses. Is there someone in your life that you never want to forget? Is it possible to always be with the people you care about every day, or every hour of the day? Of course not. But the pictures remind you of the good times and the love or friendship you have shared.

Jesus wanted us to remember him always, so he gave us something wonderful to remember him by. Does anyone know what that is? He gave us a very special meal with bread and wine. Whenever we eat and drink this bread and wine, we remember his promise to be with us and to save us. It is a promise to remember. Let's unzip our imaginations and be with Jesus and his friends at his last supper.

Meditation

Close your eyes....Wiggle your toes....Take a deep breath ....Let it out slowly....Whisper "Jesus"....Now, relax....

It is just before sunset....You slowly climb the narrow
stairway to join Jesus and his friends for dinner. The aroma
of roast lamb fills the stairwell....There is a low murmur of
voices from the room....Go through the low doorway,
ducking your head....Look around....A servant boy stretches
to light the oil lamps hanging on the walls....The dancing
light casts shadows across the room....The disciples look up
from their meal to greet you....John gets up and takes your
hand, offering you a place at the long table....Peter,
stroking his scruffy red beard, glances up and smiles,
"Welcome child!" he bellows....Sit down on the big fluffy
pillow....Scoot forward, closer to the low table....A familiar
voice calls to you....It is Jesus....Jesus stands and walks
toward you....He gives you a big hug....He says, "Thank
you for coming."

Jesus leads you to a place next to his at the long table....
Jesus bends low, whispering in your ear, "Please pass me
the basket of bread"....Jesus takes a small round piece from
the basket....It doesn't look like the bread Grandma makes
....It is flat and golden in color....He tears off a piece of the
warm bread and hands it to you, "Take this and eat it, for
this is my body"....Jesus looks lovingly into your eyes....
Place the bread in your mouth....Jesus now passes the
bread to his disciples....The room grows silent as Jesus
shares the bread with each disciple....A tear runs down
John's cheek, but he says nothing of the fear that Jesus
may be arrested tonight by his enemies....Jesus grasps the
cup of wine in front of him....He says a blessing over
it....Then, turning toward you, he says, "Drink from this.
This is a sign that we are sealing a new promise of love and
friendship. This is my blood"....Taste the sweetness from
the grapes....Jesus passes the cup to each of the disciples....
The room is so quiet that you can hear your own breathing
....Many of the disciples raise their hands in silent prayer....
A shuffling of feet behind you and the squeak of the door
hinge draw your attention....Judas slips through the door....

"I love you," whispers the gentle voice of Jesus...."My Father calls me, but I want to be with you always....I leave you this bread and wine to remember me....For now it has become my body and blood....Remember this moment always." Jesus takes your hands into his....His long fingers wrap gently around your hand....His cheeks become wet with tears....You feel the sweetness of his love and the sadness of the moment...."Do you love me?" he asks....I will give you time to be alone with Jesus....Tell him what is upon your heart.

Prayer

Jesus, Jesus, you are my light when I am afraid. When I worry I know you will take care of me. And when I have done something wrong, I know that you can bring me back to God. Thank you for giving me this special way to remember you. I love you. Amen.

It is time to leave....Say goodbye to the disciples....Give Jesus a hug....Hold on tight for a moment....Walk out of the room and down the stairs....Open your eyes and return to this room.

Discussion

- Why did the apostles think Jesus might be arrested? Why did Jesus choose this night to share the bread and wine in this special way?
- How do you think Jesus' friends felt when Jesus shared the bread and wine? Do you think they knew how special this was? How does Jesus want us to remember him?
- We have a sacrament because of the Last Supper. What is it called?

Prayer Time

Supplies: large candle; bible opened to Mt 26:26-28

Music suggestion: "Jesus, Jesus"/Hi God 2

1. Invite the children to gather in a circle. Light the candle. Read from Mt 26:26-28.

   READER: This is the word of the Lord.
   ALL: Amen.

2. Holding hands, pray the Our Father together.

3. Sing: "Jesus, Jesus" in closing.

The Gentle Touch of Jesus

Scripture: Jn 13:1-17
Feast: Days of Lent (ABC)
Music Suggestion: "I Will Never Forget You"/*Gentle Sounds*

Does Jesus think that it is important for us to help others?

Of course he does. Jesus was always helping people, and he expected us to do the same. Jesus' friends and disciples didn't always understand what Jesus wanted them to do. Does your mom or dad show you over and over how to do something right? Well, Jesus is no different. On the last night before he died, he tried to teach the disciples something. Jesus rented a room for the Passover meal and ordered all the traditional foods to be prepared, just like your family does on Thanksgiving. Let's unzip our imaginations and find out what Jesus is trying to teach his friends.

Meditation

Close your eyes....Take a deep breath....Breath out slowly ....Repeat the name "Jesus" as you do....Quiet yourself.... Relax....

You are sitting around a long table....Women are scurrying about preparing the feast....Take a deep breath....You can smell the wonderful food cooking; roast lamb, little red potatoes, bread....The light is very dim....The lantern's flickering light bounces off the walls....Jesus looks very sad ....He reaches down to his side and pats you on the shoulder....Judas arrives late, taking his place at the end of the table....John fills the cups with wine from a goatskin flask....Wine dribbles onto the tablecloth....The red stain soaks into the cloth, leaving a red pattern....Peter goes to the kitchen and brings back a tall cup of milk for you....Feel the cold milk slide down your throat....

The room is very quiet after Jesus blesses the bread and wine....Many of the disciples close their eyes, raising their arms toward heaven in prayer....You hear footsteps behind you....You open one eye....Judas is slipping out the door.... No one else seems to notice....Within a short time, voices raise and it is as though everyone is talking at once....Jesus remains very quiet....Something is on his mind....Two of the disciples begin to argue...."I am the most important!" shouts the short, dark-haired man....

"No, I am!" shouts another....Jesus pushes away from the table angrily...."Your fighting is ridiculous! It is not important who is the best or who has the most power. What is important is whether or not you are willing to help others. Are you willing to wait on others the way a servant does his master?"....The disciples grow silent....Jesus takes a towel from a nearby table, wraps it about his waist, then takes an empty basin and pitcher from the table....Jesus looks at you, "Take this pitcher and fill it with water and bring it to me"....Run outside, through the grass....Dip the pitcher into the water....Return to the house, handing the pitcher to Jesus...."Thank you my child," Jesus says gratefully....

"Please carry the bowl for me. I am going to wash the feet of my disciples," Jesus whispers in your ear....Jesus points to the floor near the feet of James....Place the bowl on the wooden floor....Water splashes out onto the floor, making a small puddle....Jesus bends down on one knee, pouring water over the feet of James....Then taking the towel from his waist, he dries the disciple's feet....One by one, Jesus leads you around the table, washing each man's feet, then drying them tenderly....

At last, it is Peter's turn....Peter does not want Jesus to wash his feet, pleading, "No, you shall never wash my feet"....Peter pulls his feet tightly under the weight of his body...."This is the job of a servant," Peter protests....Jesus places his hand on Peter's shoulder, looking into Peter's eyes...."I know that you do not understand what I am doing, but in time you will....Peter, unless I wash you, you will have no part of me"....Peter slowly lowers his feet into the bowl....

Jesus now turns to you, taking the bowl from your hand and placing it on the floor...."I am going to wash your feet now." Jesus invites you to sit. He removes the shoes from your feet....Bits of sand fall to the wooden floor. Gently, Jesus guides your feet into the waiting bowl....Jesus smiles, then pours the cool water over your feet....You shiver a little as the water splashes onto your legs....Jesus lifts your feet into his lap....He wraps your feet in his towel....The towel is soft and warm on your feet...."Do you know why I have washed the feet of my friends?" he questions you...."I want to teach each of you how important it is for you to be willing to serve others. I have given you an example that you should do for others as I have done for you."

Jesus, sitting back on his heels, looks into your eyes...."Are you willing to wait on people and always do whatever possible to help people in need? Will you follow my example of serving others?" Jesus asks....Jesus sits in silence now, waiting for your answer....

I give you a few moments to be alone with Jesus....Tell him what is on your heart....

Prayer

Jesus, when you washed my feet I learned the importance of doing for others. Sometimes it is hard for me to always think of others first, putting their needs before my own. When I forget at times, remind me, Lord, to follow your example. Amen.

It is time for you to leave....Wrap your arms around Jesus' neck....Jesus whispers, "Goodbye for now"....Turn and walk through the door....Open your eyes and return to this room.

Discussion

- Why do you think Jesus washed his disciples' feet?
- Why was Peter so upset with Jesus?
- How does Jesus expect us to follow his example?

Jesus Goes to the Park to Pray

Scripture: Mk 14:32-42
Feast: Days of Lent (ABC)
Music Suggestion: "Without You, Lord"/*Gentle Sounds*

Have you ever felt lonely and very, very sad? The world seems empty sometimes, doesn't it? Do you think Jesus ever felt lonely and sad? When?

There was a night that Jesus felt all the loneliness and sadness that the world could hold. Jesus knew that he was going to be put to death, and, like us, he was afraid. Jesus begged his Father to change his mind. Have your parents ever asked you to do something that was very, very difficult? Have you ever begged your parents to change their minds?

Meditation

Close your eyes....Wiggle your toes....Take a deep breath ....Let it out slowly....Whisper "Jesus"....Relax....

The Passover meal is over....Jesus leads you and the disciples from the upper room out into the quiet streets of Jerusalem....John moves ahead of the small band, a rusty lantern swinging back and forth on his arm....Light speckles the cobblestone streets....Jesus walks with his head down, sadness covering his face....The quiet shuffling of feet is the only sound you hear....The yowling of a cat shatters the silence....Jesus leads you through the gate of the city toward the Garden of Gethsemane....

Jesus hesitates at the gate of the garden...."Wait here while I go into the garden and pray," Jesus tells his friends.... Before you can lower yourself onto the grassy knoll, Jesus speaks again, "Peter, John, James, and you, my child," Jesus says, pointing to you, "please stay with me"....Jesus' shoulders droop, his footsteps heavy....Jesus reaches out his hand for yours....His touch is gentle....His fingers fold about your hand, not clasping, just holding, enjoying your touch ....Jesus wipes a small tear from his eye....Looking down at you, he explains, "I am feeling very sad tonight. I shall not come here again"....Jesus stops, calling out, "Wait here for me. Do not leave me alone tonight"....

Jesus walks further into the garden, falling onto his knees.... His broad shoulders hang heavy as though he carries the weight of the world upon his back....Jesus falls forward, burying his face in the cold, hard ground....Jesus breaks into tears....The sound of sorrow, the sound of loneliness, the sound of fear fill the night....Jesus' body shakes with the depth of his sobs....Move closer to Jesus....Lie down next to him....Put your face close to his....Hear his sadness.... Touch his hand....Let him know you love him....Touch his sadness....Jesus begs his Father in heaven, "Father, Father, everything is possible for you. If it is possible, take this cup of sorrow from me." Stillness and acceptance settle over him....Looking to heaven, he speaks again, "Father, I will do your will, not mine."

Jesus slowly raises himself from the ground....Standing in silence, he takes your hand in his once again....Walk down the gentle slope where James, John, and Peter lie sleeping ....Jesus looks at his friends, shaking his head....He whispers his sorrow, "You could not watch with me even one hour"....Jesus walks away slowly, dropping to his knees ....He continues to pray, "If this cup of sorrow cannot pass unless I drink it....your will be done"....Jesus returns to his disciples....Sadly, he sees they are fast asleep....He looks down at you, his eyes damp with tears, "They do not understand what the night will bring." Jesus kneels in prayer, leaning against a huge boulder; his hands folded, his eyes looking upward, he slowly repeats his pleadings, "Father, if possible, let this cup pass from me"....The moonlight casts eerie shadows across the garden....Clouds move across the night sky....

Only you and Jesus remain awake....He moves quietly toward you....His walk is slow....He is standing beside you....His cheeks glisten in the moonlight, wet with tears.... Leaning against a tree trunk, Jesus lowers himself to the ground....Take your hand and wipe away his tears....Hold his tears in the palm of your hand....Place your hand over your heart, allowing his tears to soak into your clothing.... Jesus smiles gently at you and begins to speak, "I must leave you soon. It is my Father's will that I must suffer and die so that mankind will be saved. I must obey my Father" ....He turns away from you, walking toward the garden gates....Run down the sloping hillside....Try to catch up with Jesus....In the distance you hear angry voices.... Burning torches light the sky....Catch up with Jesus....Walk with him as he faces his enemies. I will give you time to speak to Jesus....

Prayer
Dearest Jesus, I love you. I wish I could take away your loneliness and sadness. I will always remember holding your tears in my hand. Forgive me, Lord, for those times that I have not been willing to obey. Help me to follow your example.

It is time to leave Jesus....He knows that you are with him in your heart....Open your eyes and return to this room.

Discussion

- How did Jesus feel in the garden? Why?
- What did he ask of God? Why did he ask this?
- How do you think the disciples felt each time Jesus returned to wake them?

Rejoice! Jesus Has Risen!

Scripture: Mt 28:1-10; Mk 16:1-8; Lk 24:1-11
Feast: Easter (ABC)
Music Suggestion: "We Believe in You"/*Gentle Sounds*

How do you think Jesus' friends felt when they discovered the tomb empty? They must have been frightened. If you had been with Mary of Magdala and the other women who found the tomb empty, how would you feel? Let's unzip our imaginations and find out what happened.

Meditation

Close your eyes....Stretch your fingers....Take a deep breath....Breathe out slowly....Whisper "Jesus"....Relax....

It is early morning on the third day following Jesus' death....The sun is just rising above the rooftops....Roosters signal the beginning of day, "Cockle-doodle-do"....The women who followed Jesus from Galilee are going to the tomb to anoint his body with oils. Mary of Magdala notices you and invites you to join them....Grab a jacket....The early morning air is chilly....Mary hands you a bottle of oil....Walk slowly up the steep hillside....Be careful not to spill the oil....One of the women asks, "Who will move the big stone away from the entrance to the tomb so that we can go inside?"....

After some time you arrive at the top of the hill....
Overnight, flowers have bloomed....Red tulips, yellow
daisies, and white lilies wave their heads in the gentle
breeze....Butterflies flit from flower to flower....You have
never seen so many butterflies....Look to the right....There
is Jesus' tomb....The stone is rolled back. "Who has done
this?" questions one of the women....Mary motions for you
to join her at her side...."Let's look inside," she suggests....
One careful step at a time, you and Mary peek inside the
tomb....It's empty!....Nothing remains except for the burial
cloths....You hear a stirring from within the tomb....A bright
light shines, dazzling your eyes....A young man, dressed
entirely in white, speaks to you...."Why are you looking in a
tomb for someone who is alive? He isn't here! Jesus is not
dead. Remember, he told you that he would be handed over
to people who would crucify him, but on the third day he
would rise from the dead....Jesus has been raised up"....Not
understanding this, Mary begins to cry, "They have taken
Jesus away."

Three of the women run off down the hillside toward
Jerusalem...."They are going to tell everyone that Jesus'
body is gone," Mary explains....You and Mary walk over to
a large olive tree....You sit beneath its huge branches....
Mary cries softly....She turns around and sees a man
standing there. She thinks that it is the man who cares for
the garden....The man speaks softly, "Why are you crying?
Who are you looking for?" he asks. "Where is Jesus?" Mary
demands....Gently, the man touches Mary's shoulder,
whispering, "Mary!"....Mary wipes her tears away....
Looking deeply into the man's eyes, she cries out, "Jesus!"
....Look at the man....He speaks to you, calling your name,
"Did you think that I had left you?" he asks....It really is
Jesus! His body is no longer in the cave because Jesus is
alive!

The birds sing....Baby bunnies run among the tall blades of
grass....Breathe in the sweet fragrance of flowers....Mary

runs off to tell her friends how special Jesus really is. God brought his son, Jesus, back to life once again. You and Jesus stand alone in the beautiful hillside....The sun shines warmly now....Jesus holds out his loving arms to you....Feel his arms wrap around you...."I will always keep my promises," Jesus whispers in your ear....Imagine that you are very small....Climb up onto his lap....Feel his love and protection. Take this time to talk to Jesus....Speak to him from your heart. I will leave you with Jesus.

Prayer

Dear Jesus, through our imaginations we witnessed the events of the first Easter morning when you rose from the dead to a new life. Through you, Jesus, we are all going to have life everlasting. Help me to live my life with hope. Help me to be a good witness in the world to all that you did and said. Amen.

It is time to leave Jesus....Tell Jesus goodbye for now.... Give him one last hug....Walk away....Open your eyes and return to this room.

Discussion

- Have you ever been afraid when you thought that you were left alone?
- How do you think Mary felt when she recognized Jesus?
- When you went to the tomb and found it empty, what did you think happened?
- How does your family celebrate Easter?

71

One Touch Is Enough!

Scripture: Jn 20:19-31
Feast: Second Sunday of Easter (A)
Music Suggestion: "When You Seek Me"/*Gentle Sounds*

If Jesus walked into this room, right this minute, would you believe it was really Jesus? What would it take to prove to you that it was really Jesus? If you touched him, would be able to tell that it was Jesus?

When Jesus was on earth, people would often reach out and touch him. It was a touch they would always remember. It was a touch so filled with love they could feel it all over. Sometimes it is hard to believe in something if we cannot see it.

We can't reach out and touch Jesus with our hands today, but we can always feel close to him. Let's unzip our imaginations, traveling back to time of Jesus. It is Easter Sunday evening. You are one of Jesus' disciples. Will one touch be enough for you to believe?

Meditation

Close your eyes....Stretch out your fingertips....Wiggle your toes....Relax....

One by one, you have crept into an old building standing on the edge of the city....Slowly you ease yourself up the old

72

wooden stairway so that no one will hear you....Creeeak! groans the step....A chill goes through you....Ssshhh!....You feel your heart pounding against your chest....Roman soldiers cover the streets like the web of a spider....You never know where they will be until its too late....They are hunting for the friends of Jesus, searching everywhere....

You are now inside the darkened room. Peter moves over to the door, pulling the lock shut....James closes the window shutters, shutting out the last glimmer of light.... You are afraid to even light a candle....The room is very crowded....People speak in whispers....You hear a woman sobbing....A voice from the darkness speaks...."The tomb was empty!"....

You huddle in the darkness, feeling all alone....Suddenly, Jesus is standing in front of you!...."Peace, my child," Jesus whispers....Jesus knows that you are frightened....He reaches out to comfort you....His hand almost touches yours....He shows you his hands and his side....Jesus looks directly at you now, the light from the candle flickering across his face...."Do you believe?" he asks....(*Pause for a moment.*)....You believe! This is Jesus!....You spring to your feet, filled with joy....Then, as suddenly as he appeared, he leaves....You have seen Jesus! He is alive!.... You look around for your friend, Thomas....Peter tells you that Thomas has not arrived....

Later, the same evening, you walk with a few disciples to Thomas' home, crouching in the shadows....The disciples tell Thomas what they have seen....Thomas stands shaking his head....He does not believe....You tell Thomas about the wounds in Jesus' hands, the wound in his side.... Thomas turns his back and walks away from you...."I'll believe when I can touch the hands of Jesus myself....and put my hand into the gash in his side"....You try one more time to make Thomas believe....He leaves shaking his head in disbelief....

One week has past....You are once again locked in the small room....Thomas sits close by your side in the darkness ....Clatter! Crash!....Listen to the footsteps of the Roman soldiers in the street below....Fear tickles your spine....Grab Thomas' hand....The candle flickers....Voices are stilled.... Hear the quiet....Someone is standing beside you....It is Jesus!...."Peace, my children. Do not be afraid," Jesus commands....You feel safe now....Nothing can harm you, Jesus is beside you....

Jesus turns to your friend Thomas, "Touch the marks on my hands and feel the wound in my side"....Thomas slowly reaches forward, barely touching the hands of Jesus...."My Lord, My God," Thomas says, falling to his knees.... "Thomas, you believed because you saw, but blessed are people who believed but did not see me."

You feel like laughing, shouting....Happiness lights up the room....You will always remember this moment....Jesus takes your hand into his and holds it tightly for a moment.... Can you feel his touch?....Feel his long fingers wrap around your hand....You feel love....Love that starts at your fingertips and rushes to your toes....You want to shout, "Jesus is here!"

Jesus looks within your eyes, asking, "Do you believe, my child?" I will leave you alone with Jesus to his question.

Prayer
Jesus, I do believe in you. I love you. Help me to always grow in faith and love. Amen.

Jesus tells you that it is time for you to return....He bends low, picking you up in his arms....Give Jesus a big hug.... Turn and walk away....Open your eyes and return to this room. You will remember his touch forever....One touch is enough!

Discussion

- Is it difficult to believe in things we have not seen?
- If someone you trust tells you something, will you believe it?
- Do your believe that you can see Jesus with your heart? How?

Activity

1. Select a panel of four judges. Ask two children at a time to come forward. The first child makes a statement about something she/he has seen. The judges say, "I believe it!" or "I doubt it." Ask the rest of the children for their vote.

2. Explain that we see Jesus not with our eyes but with our hearts and that some people doubt this kind of seeing.

A Walk in Faith

Scripture: Lk 24:13-31
Feast: Third Sunday of Easter (A)
Music Suggestion: "When You Seek Me"/*Gentle Sounds*

Have any of your friends ever promised to call you and then didn't? Did you feel left out and sad? Two of Jesus' friends felt just like that after Jesus died. They felt abandoned, as though Jesus didn't care about them any more. You know how that feels. Jesus promised them that he would never leave them, and then he died on the cross. There was a great deal of talk about Jesus rising from the dead, the empty tomb, and even some people said that they saw Jesus! Two of his friends gave up on seeing Jesus and decided to return to their homes in Emmaus. These two men had a surprise coming! Jesus never forgets his friends.

Let's unzip our imaginations and travel back to a warm spring day and see just what is going to happen.

Meditation

Close your eyes....Wiggle your fingers....Take in a deep breath....Let out the air, whispering "Jesus" as you do.... Relax....

You are walking down a dirt road....The dirt fills your sandals with each step....It is three days since Jesus died and you feel very sad....Jesus was your best friend....Now he is gone forever....Kick a rock on the roadway....Look ahead....There are two men on the road ahead....You have seen them with Jesus before....Look closely at the men. Do you know them? ....Yes, one of them is your friend Cleopas!....Run ahead to meet them....You call out, "Cleopas, wait for me"....

Cleopas, his shoulders bent, greets you with a warm hug. His friend, a tall man with dark hair, shakes your hand.... Cleopas explains that they are returning to their homes in Emmaus now that Jesus is gone....You can feel their sadness; you will miss Jesus too....Walk along listening to the men speak of Jesus and how lonely they are going to be....Wipe a tear from your cheek....

Turning a bend in the road, another man joins your group....He turns to you, asking, "What are you talking about?"...."Haven't you heard what happened?" Cleopas interrupts. "Our Master, Jesus, died on a cross. He was buried three days ago. Today some women went to his tomb to anoint the body. But the tomb was empty. Now we do not know what to think"....Tell the stranger about your friend, Jesus....(*Pause.*)....The man listens to every word, shaking his head in wonder...."Is this why you seem so sad?" he asks....The stranger offers you his hand....You feel him squeeze your hand....As you continue your journey toward Emmaus, the stranger begins to speak to you about God...."But why did Jesus die?" Cleopas interrupts....The stranger looks at the two men and shakes his head, "You do not know very much....Jesus had to die to bring new life to people....I know that you have heard this before".... These words sound familiar to you....You question silently, "How does he know so much about God?"

The sun is beginning to set....The time has passed quickly ....You are now in front of Cleopas' house....The stranger shakes hands with your friends and pats you on the back, offering his goodbyes....Instead of saying goodbye, Cleopas invites the stranger to supper, saying that he wants to hear more stories about God....You are happy he is not leaving ....Rush through the doorway to the house, making your way to the kitchen....Light the lamp and clear off the table ....Look through the cupboards hurriedly, placing bowls on the long wooden table: a few fish, some fruit and nuts, a fresh loaf of bread and some wine....

Cleopas and his friend take their places at the table....The guest invites you to sit beside him, patting the pillows.... Cleopas lights the table candle and offers thanks to God for the food. The visitor smiles warmly...."Tell us more stories from scripture," Cleopas begs with excitement....The stranger tells stories of Noah and Jonah, wonderful stories about God....Pass the basket of warm bread....The visitor takes the bread from your hands, blesses it and hands you a piece first....Place the warm bread upon your tongue.... Next, he hands the bread to the two men across the table.... Your mouth drops open in disbelief....This is Jesus!....Jesus did come back just as he said he would! You have been talking with Jesus and didn't recognize him! Your face turns red with embarrassment....

Jesus takes your hand in his, leading you out into the garden. The evening air carries the sweet fragrance of rose blossoms ....You and Jesus are all alone....Jesus leans close, whispering, "I will never leave you." Jesus folds one arm around you, holding you close to his side....My child, is there something you wish to talk over with me?"....I will leave you alone to talk to Jesus. Listen to his words of love....

(Pause for half a minute or until the children become restless.)

Prayer
Jesus, I love you. I know that I can always turn to you with my worries and problems. Thank you for your love. Amen.

It is time to leave Jesus....Give Jesus a hug....Wave goodbye to your friends....Walk through the door....Open your eyes and return to this room.

Discussion

- Is Jesus alive today? (*Yes*)
- Where can we find Jesus? (*In each other, ourselves, church, the Eucharist*)
- How did you recognize Jesus?

Prayer Time

1. Invite the children to share their experience on the road to Emmaus.

2. Dim the lights, lighting only one candle. Break a piece of bread, pass it to the child next to you, then invite the children to share the bread with each other, saying, "Jesus is the Bread of Life, (*Name*)."

3. Pray the following:

   LEADER:
   Dear Jesus,
       we pray for all those who have lost hope,
       that they will find you.
   We pray for those who find it hard to believe in you.
   We pray for those preparing to receive you
       in communion for the first time.
   Lord,
       you are the Bread of Life.
   Help us remember that You are always with us.
   CHILDREN: Lord, you are the Bread of Life. Amen.

Going Fishing with Jesus

Scripture: Jn 21:1-19
Feast: Third Sunday of Easter (C)
Music Suggestion: "By Name I Have Called You"/*Gentle Sounds*

Materials: rock, fishing pole or picture of one
Optional: blue blanket or fabric, a few pieces of charcoal

(*Show the fishing pole.*) Can anyone name a close friend of Jesus that might use a fishing pole? (*Show the rock.*) This is a clue about his name. Jesus called him "the rock." He was the leader of the disciples. Does anyone know his name?

Jesus gave Peter his name because he is like a rock on which the church was built. Peter believed in Jesus and he told other people who told other people who told other people until someone told me and I told you. Peter was the first leader of the church. One day Jesus asked Peter a question that brought tears to Peter's eyes.

A long time ago we heard a story about four fishermen. Peter was one of the fishermen. These fishermen followed Jesus and helped him teach people about God's love. When Jesus died on the cross, the fishermen were very sad because they thought they would never see Jesus again. But this story has a surprise ending. Let's unzip our imaginations and join Peter, the leader of the disciples. It is a few days after Jesus died on the cross. Peter has decided to take the boat out and go fishing.

Meditation

Close your eyes....Wiggle your toes....Take a deep breath ....Let it out slowly....Whisper "Jesus"....Now, relax....

It is early evening....A very sad Peter rows his fishing boat out to sea....James grabs an oar, helping Peter row the bobbing boat....Curl up in the bottom of the boat....All night long the disciples take turns throwing the nets out into the cold, dark water....But each time, they pull up an empty net....Early the next morning, as the sun is rising above the mountaintops, you notice a figure standing on the beach....He looks familiar....Peter squints his eyes, asking, "Who is that standing on the shore?"....The rising sun leaves fingers of darkness, making it hard to see...."It looks likes Jesus!....It must be my imagination, or is it?" you question yourself....You decide to say nothing....The man on shore calls out, "Did you catch anything?"...."No!" the disciples answer...."Put your nets down into the water on the right side of the boat and you will catch some fish," the man instructs Peter....Peter grumbles, "Who does this guy think he is?....Oh, well, we've got nothing to lose....Child, help lower the net"....Struggle with the weight of the net.... The rough ropes sting your hands....Now you understand why Peter's hands are so rough....The net sinks into the water....Quickly the net tugs at the side of the boat....The net is full!....James and Andrew pull the bulging cargo onto the deck....Look again at the figure standing on the beach.... You recognize him. It is Jesus!....Tell Peter your amazing discovery....He strains his eyes...."No, it can't be. We will go to shore and take a closer look!" Peter barks.

The bottom of the boat hits the sandy shore....James helps you down from the boat....The water slaps at your bare

legs....Wade ashore....Feel the shells cutting into your feet
....Straight ahead, on the beach, a charcoal fire warms the
early morning air....Fish hanging from sticks sizzle and pop
above the coals....Jesus waits nearby....He smiles at you....It
is so wonderful to see Jesus again!....Run to meet him....
Peter rubs his eyes in disbelief....Jesus, turning to Peter,
calls out, "Bring some of the fish you caught and put them
on the fire"....Peter, his mouth open, walks back to the
boat and gathers fish in a small net...."Come and have
some breakfast," Jesus offers....No one asks "Who are
you?" because now they all seem to know that it is the
Lord....Jesus breaks the bread into small pieces, giving you
the first bite, then Peter and the others....Jesus passes a fish
hot from the fire to everyone....Eat quickly....You are
hungry....Your tummy is full of fresh fried fish and warm
soft bread....You sit curled at Jesus' feet....The fire crackles
....Small puffs of smoke lift into the air....Jesus pats you on
the back....He watches in silence as Peter finishes the last of
his meal, then wipes his mouth on the back of his arm....
Jesus turns to Peter...."Peter, do you truly love me?" Jesus
asks Peter....Peter stammers, reaching out to touch the
hand of Jesus, "Yes, Lord, you know that I love you"....
Jesus answers, "Feed my lambs"....Poking at the fire, Jesus
asks Peter again, "Do you love me?"....Peter looks very sad
....His eyes spill tears down his weather-beaten face....Peter's
voice is chocked with emotion, "You know I love you, Jesus"
....Jesus looks thoughtfully into the flames, then responds,
"Feed my sheep"....Jesus asks Peter a third time, "Do you
love me?"....You wonder why Jesus is questioning Peter in
this way....

Peter sits by the fire, hiding his face in his arms....Jesus
pulls you close to his side and, taking Peter's hand, he
explains, "I have taken care of you....Now I want you to
take care of all the people who do not know me. Lead them
to me"....Jesus turns his attention to you. Bending lower,
he whispers your name, then asks, "Do you love me?"

I will leave you alone with Jesus for a few moments....Tell Jesus all that is upon your heart....

Prayer

Dear Jesus, I believe that you are alive and with us through your Spirit. Thank you for calling me to be your special friend. Help me to bring your message of love and peace to everyone I meet. Amen.

It is time to leave Jesus....Say goodbye to your friend.... Walk away, your feet digging into the soft sand....Turn and wave goodbye....Open your eyes and return to this room.

Discussion

- Whom did the disciples find on the beach?
- What did Jesus ask Peter? Why do you think Jesus asked this question so many times?
- What did he tell Peter to do? What does Jesus want us to do?

Activity: Dramatization

Invite the children to act out the bible story as you read it. You will need: Jesus, a group of disciples, and Peter. Designate a blue blanket or cloth to be the sea; set a few charcoal briquettes a short distance from the "sea" to be the charcoal fire. After you read a line of dialog in the story, have the person or group repeat the words. Continue reading in this way. Ask the children to move to the sea or to the fire, according to the outline of the story.

No Easy Road

Scripture: Jn 10:11-18
Feast: Fourth Sunday of Easter (ABC)
Music Suggestion: "Psalm of the Good Shepherd"/*Gentle Sounds*
OR "Shepherd Me, O God"/*Instruments of Peace*

Do you have a pet? What happens when you call your pet's name? Have you ever seen sheep or lambs? Who takes care of sheep and lambs? (*Spend a few minutes talking about sheep and shepherds.*)

Jesus talks about himself as a shepherd. Jesus says that he is a good shepherd, caring for each of us like a shepherd cares for his sheep. He keeps us safe and gives us everything we need. Jesus knows each by name. Let's unzip our imaginations and listen to what Jesus has to tell us about being a good shepherd.

Meditation

Close your eyes....Take a deep breath....Let the breath out slowly....Whisper "Jesus"....Relax....

You are in a grassy field, far away from the city. The land is rough....Huge rocks jut out of the earth....It is early evening ....Sheep and their lambs graze on the last blades of grass on the nearly barren field....A tiny black lamb walks over to your side....Bend over and pet the lamb....Feel the softness of the lamb's wool....A voice calls out from beyond the trees

...."The new lamb thinks that you are his shepherd"....Look into the rays of the setting sun....The figure moving toward you is only a shadow....As he draws closer you recognize the voice....It is Jesus!....He calls you by name...."Watch out for the baby lamb. He is about to wander off," Jesus warns....Run and catch the lamb....Bring the lamb back and place it at your feet....Jesus holds out his arms to greet you ....He is smiling and happy...."Come and sit with me for a while," Jesus says, smiling down at you....Hand in hand, you and Jesus walk to a small clump of trees....The little black lamb follows closely at your heels....

Jesus sits down leaning against the tree....He pats the ground next to him...."Come and sit next to me," Jesus tells you...."I want to tell you a story about a shepherd." The little lamb curls up in a tight little ball at your feet....It shivers as the cold night covers the evening with a mist....Take off your coat and cover the lamb....Jesus smiles, wrapping his warm arms around you...."You are being a good shepherd for that little lamb," he says....

"Sheep are like the shepherd's special friends. They follow the shepherd, and he protects them from wild animals. He makes sure they have enough to eat and that they have water to drink. If the little lambs are tired, sometimes the shepherd carries them. The sheep and their shepherd get to know each other very well"....Jesus reaches down and pets the tiny lamb, "Just as you care for this little lamb, the shepherd must take care of a whole flock of sheep." Settle back against Jesus....Jesus removes his own coat, draping it around your shoulders....You quickly snuggle into the warmth of Jesus' arms.

"Once upon a time there was a shepherd taking care of his sheep....His name was William....For many years William worked hard protecting his sheep from wolves and others who would want to steal or harm them, raising his family, and working for God. William thought that he knew everything there was to know about being a shepherd.

"At long last he saved enough money to buy his own little farm. He planted a garden. He bought some chickens and a cow, and he let sheep graze in his front yard. His garden grew, his cow gave milk, and his sheep had baby lambs.

"One day, a terrible storm came up. Lightening flashed. Thunder boomed. It rained and rained. William worried about his farm animals but decided they were safe in the barn. Then he heard the bleating of a lamb. He went outside to find a lamb lying on the ground. The lamb was shaking and quivering. When it thundered, the lamb shook a little harder. William picked up the lamb, dried it off, held it for a short time, and then sent it out into the field again.

"Later in the evening, William went out to feed the animals. In the darkness, he tripped over a small figure lying on his porch. The little black lamb had died—scared to death by the storm. Tears cloud William's eyes when he talks about the little lamb. He tells everyone, 'I should have been a better shepherd. If I would have held him a little longer, until he felt safe, my lamb would have lived. I needed to give just a little more of my time.'"....Jesus leans forward, rubbing his hands to keep warm...."I know that story made you feel sad but I want you to understand that I am your good shepherd, my child. I will always protect you and love you. I will never leave you alone. I will always know the sound of your voice when you call. Just as you would care for this little lamb, I shall always care for you."

You smile at Jesus, feeling safe and secure....Jesus looks into your eyes and asks, "Is there someone or something in your life that you need to give 'just a little more time' to?" I will leave you alone with Jesus, your good shepherd.

Prayer

Jesus, I am like the little lamb and you are my loving shepherd. Help me to always answer when you call my name and follow wherever you lead me. Amen.

It is time to leave Jesus....Pick up the little lamb and place it in Jesus' waiting arms....Say goodbye....Get up and begin to walk away....Open your eyes and return to this room.

Discussion

• What did William learn about being a good shepherd? How is Jesus our good shepherd?

• If you could give just "a little more time" to someone or something in your life, who or what would it be?

Prayer Time

Supplies: bible, candle
Optional music: "My Shepherd Is the Lord"/We Belong to God

1. Gather the children into a circle. Light a candle. Invite the children to think of someone who helps them when they have a problem.

   LEADER: Would anyone like to share the name of the person and explain the help you received? *(Invite the children to ask Jesus to bless this person in a special way.)*

   LEADER: Jesus we ask you to bless *(Name)* in a special way.

   CHILDREN: Thank you, Jesus.

2. Open the bible and read Jn 10:11-18. Holding hands, pray the Our Father. Close with "My Shepherd Is the Lord."

I Will Come Back to You

Scripture: Jn 14:23-29
Feast: Sixth Sunday of Easter (C)
Music Suggestion: "I Will Never Forget You"/*Gentle Sounds*
    OR "Spirit of God"/*Instruments of Peace*

Has anyone ever wanted to do something good for
someone else? Perhaps you wanted to surprise your mom
or dad by fixing breakfast for them or cleaning the house
while they were at work. Sometimes we may see an older
person or little child having problems and we really desire to
help out. How do you feel when you follow your feelings to
do something nice for others? Why do you suppose we feel
the urge to do something nice?

The Holy Spirit nudges us to do good things. Let me
explain the Holy Spirit this way. Can you see the wind?
How do we know it is there? We feel it in different ways.
We cannot see the Holy Spirit, but the Spirit of Jesus is in
us and helps us. The Holy Spirit is with us through our
baptism. The Spirit can fill us with joy and happiness. The
Spirit is like the breath of God.

One day Jesus made us a promise that the Holy Spirit
would always be with us. After Jesus' death, the apostles
were very frightened. They feared that Jesus' enemies
would find them also. They felt as though Jesus had
abandoned them even though Jesus appeared once before
to some of his disciples. When Jesus did appear to them

once again, he wanted to set their minds at rest, and he greeted them with "Peace be with you!" Let's unzip our imaginations and experience the peace of Jesus.

Meditation

Close your eyes....Shrug your shoulders....Take a deep breath....Let it out slowly....Whisper "Jesus"....Relax....

You sit in silence in the darkened upper room. Windows are boarded shut....The air is heavy and stale....One tiny candle lights the crowded room....It seems like a bad dream; everyone is caught in the shadows of the night....They speak in hushed voices....Peter sobs quietly, "My friend, Jesus, is going away and I am afraid that I may never see him again".... Place your hand on Peter's shoulder....Feel Peter's sadness....Remember how you felt when your friend moved away or someone you loved died....Tears form in your eyes....Wipe your eyes....There is someone standing in front of you....It is Jesus!....He places his hand above your head, "Do not be afraid, Child. May my peace be with you"....Suddenly, the room brightens with the light of Christ....Your worries disappear and your tears turn to smiles....Jesus smiles down at you....He moves quickly among the apostles, reassuring them that he will never leave them alone....Peter collapses at Jesus' feet....Jesus takes Peter's rough calloused hands in his, helping him to his feet, "I love you, Peter," he says gently....Turning his attention to the others, he speaks once again...."Where two or three are gathered in my name, I am with you. You will never be alone again. My Father is going to send the Holy Spirit, who will teach you everything and remind you of all that I have said"....

Jesus walks through the crowded room, spreading a feeling of well being....At last he comes back to you. Bending low on one knee he calls you by name, "Never be afraid, my child. Let your heart be at peace. I promise you that you will never be alone. I will always be with you"....A feeling of love for others fills your heart....Taking you into his arms, he whispers, "Follow your feelings to do good things".... Holding you close he adds, "I love you"....Quiet, peace and happiness fill you from head to toe....I will give you a few minutes to talk to Jesus. Speak to him with your heart....

Prayer
Jesus, sometimes I forget to follow your "nudge" to help others. For all the times it is difficult for me to act in loving ways—paying attention in school, avoid fighting, and sharing with others—fill me with your Spirit, Jesus. May I live in your peace forever. Amen.

It is time to leave now....Say goodbye to the apostles....Give Jesus a hug....Turn and walk through the doorway....Open your eyes and return to this room.

Discussion

- What did Jesus promise us? How does the Holy Spirit help us?
- How can we show others the "peace of Christ?"

Prayer Time

Supplies: bible opened to Jn 14:23-29, large candle, music tape, "Come Holy Spirit"/In the Spirit We Belong

1. Invite the children to form a circle around the lighted candle. Read from the bible, first raising it above your head reverently then returning it to a place of honor.

   LEADER: May the world become a more peaceful place, where people learn to forgive. May the

90

world be filled with the joy of the Lord, where
we take time to enjoy each other's presence.

2. Offer a sign of peace to the person next to you. Now,
invite the children to offer the sign of peace to each
other.

3. Close with "Come Holy Spirit."

The Breath of Life

Scripture: Jn 20:19-23
Feast: Pentecost (ABC)
Music Suggestion: "Spirit of God"/*Instruments of Peace*
  OR "Only a Shadow"/*Gentle Sounds*

Turn on an electric fan. Allow the a few moments to enjoy the gentle breeze. Then explain:

Most of us can feel the breeze, can't we? We know that it is coming from the fan, but we cannot see the breeze, only feel it. The Holy Spirit that Jesus promised is just like the air coming from the fan. We feel it coming from deep within our hearts, but we are unable to see it. We feel his Holy Spirit; it gives us courage and strength to do what is right. Jesus promised his friends that he would send them the Holy Spirit to enable them to continue his work, giving them the strength to do what is right.

After Jesus' death, his friends were very frightened, going and coming only in the dark of night, sneaking through the shadows to reach the stairway to the upper room. They gathered together, waiting and hoping Jesus would once again appear. Let's unzip our imaginations, joining our friends in the upper room to experience the coming of the Holy Spirit.

Darken the room, lighting one candle. Ask a helper to stand among the children, greeting them with, "Peace be with you!"

Meditation

Close your eyes....Relax....Shrug your shoulders....Take a deep breath....Let it out slowly....

It is nightfall....Darkness begins to cover the day with its shadows....You are moving through the darkened streets, looking first to the right and then to the left....No one is following you....You slowly, quietly, make your way up the creaking stairway....At last, Peter opens the small door to the room....

Candles flicker....Shadows dance across the crowded room, bouncing off the frightened faces....The door creaks and whines behind you....More people come into the room.... The air is heavy and stale....The windows are boarded shut....People speak in soft whispers, hoping the night air will not carry the sound of their voices to the street far below.

You recognize Mary, the mother of Jesus. She sits quietly by the door....A tear falls from her cheek....John stands closely by, his hand on Mary's shoulder....Walk over to Mary....Wrap your arms about her shoulders....Take a moment to speak to Mary. *(Pause for 15-20 seconds.)*

A knock on the door shatters the quiet....Move to a darkened corner of the room....Peter opens the door.... James the apostle makes his way into the room...."The Roman soldiers are searching the houses for us....We need to be very careful tonight," James says in a loud whisper.... Peter moves to the light of a candle, his rough red beard framing his face, "If only Jesus were here"....

The words of Peter hang in the air....Without warning, the sound of surging wind fills the room, reminding you of the whistling sound of wind whipping through treetops....The whole house shakes beneath your feet....Doors rattle.... Boards on the windows break, setting the hurricane winds free....The candles and lanterns flicker, then die out....You feel the wind rushing through your hair....Before you can move or speak, light covers the room....You can see light, in the shape of flames, above everyone's head....Looking up, you see the tongues of fire above your own head....

No longer do you feel afraid....A calm settles over everyone in the room....Peace covers you like a warm blanket on a cold winter's night....Feelings of happiness and joy start at your toes and flow to your heart....This is like the happiness of Christmas morning and birthday surprises....Let the feeling of joy fill you all the way to the top....Enjoy the moment....

"It is the Holy Spirit!" Peter shouts...."Jesus kept his promise!" John adds excitedly. People move about the room joyfully, laughing, dancing....Peter takes your hands and leads you to the center of the room...."Be happy, my child. The Spirit of the Lord is truly with you!" he shouts.... You feel the warm breath of God rush through you....

The windows and doors stand open now....Everyone is rushing to the streets below....You look out the window....A crowd has gathered....You leave the window, rushing down the stairs into the starlit night....There is dancing in the street....You begin to feel the strength and courage to tell others about the happiness you feel, the love you feel for Jesus, for your family and friends....The Holy Spirit will help you to show love to others even when that is difficult. Take a moment to feel the happiness....

It is time to leave now....Say goodbye to everyone....Give Mary a hug....Remember, the Holy Spirit is within us when we love, when we share happiness and peace....Open your eyes and enter this room....

Discussion

- Would someone like to share your experiences in the upper room?
- Think of a time when you might need the Holy Spirit's help. It may be when you need to make a tough decision or know the right thing to do and you need the strength to do it.
- Can anyone share a time you might have needed the help of the Holy Spirit?

Prayer Time

> LEADER: Let us now pray for the peace of Jesus and the coming of his Holy Spirit.
>
> RESPONSE: *(Sing verse one of "We Are One in the Spirit.")*
>
> LEADER: Let us pray that the world will become a more peaceful place.
>
> RESPONSE: *(Sing verse two of "We Are One in the Spirit.")*

Using the children's suggestions of times they feel the need for the Holy Spirit, offer prayers of petition.

> LEADER: For these needs and all the needs of your children, we pray to You, O Lord.
>
> RESPONSE: *(Repeat verse one of "We Are One in the Spirit.")*

Part III

Ordinary Time

Invitation to a Wedding

Scripture: Jn 2:1-12
Feast: Second Sunday of Ordinary Time (C)
Music Suggestion: "Canticle of the Sun"/*Instruments of Peace*
    OR "When You Seek Me"/*Gentle Sounds*

One day, Jesus received an invitation to a wedding in Cana. Has anyone ever received an invitation to a wedding? Have you ever been to a wedding? Did they run out of punch or cake? This wedding did! Mary asked her son, Jesus, to help his friends. Jesus surprised Mary with his answer. Does anyone know how Jesus answered his mother?

Is there anything you've ever wanted to do that you weren't old enough or ready to do? (*Riding a bike, wearing make-up, driving.*) Sometimes we want to do things, but the time is just not right. The first time Jesus was asked to show he was sent from God, he probably wasn't sure whether or not he was ready and he probably wasn't sure his followers were ready either. But he went ahead and helped his friends. He showed everyone—his friends, his disciples, his mother, and the people at the wedding feast—God's love. By unzipping our imaginations we will be able to receive an invitation to the wedding at Cana. I wonder what surprises Jesus will have for us today.

Meditation

Close your eyes....Wiggle your fingers....Take a deep breath ....Let it out slowly....Whisper "Jesus"....Relax....

The disciple James hands you an envelope....Break the wax seal....That's the way they used to seal envelopes in Jesus' time....You, the disciples, Jesus, and Mary have been invited to a wedding in Cana....You are excited!....Wedding parties sometimes go on for days....Mary busies herself preparing food for the party....James gets his best clothes out of the closet....Jesus packs a small knapsack for the journey....Glancing your way, he smiles, "Remember your party clothes," he chuckles....At last you begin your journey ....Everyone is in a happy mood....Jesus sings silly ditties and tells jokes, making everyone laugh....It is fun to laugh and joke with Jesus.

It is almost dusk....The setting sun casts its shadows over the countryside....Listen, there is music and laughter in the distance....Mary calls out, "There it is! We have arrived! Knock on the door, child, and let them know their wedding guests are here"....Knock as hard as you can on the thick wooden door....Does anyone hear you?....The bridegroom answers the door....Smiling, he hugs Jesus and Mary, then welcomes everyone to his home....Wonderful tall cakes, sweet cookies, and goodies of all sorts are being served....It reminds you of Christmas time at home....Everyone is happy and laughing. After several hours of party and music, Mary speaks quietly in Jesus' ear, "They do not have any more wine"....Jesus frowns, then questions, "Why are you telling me about this? It is not time for people to know who I am"....His answer surprises both you and Mary.

Mary walks over to the six large wine jars, tipping them on their side....A small dribble of wine forms a lacy pattern.... There is very little wine and so many people....Mary beckons for you...."Child, go to those who are serving and tell them to do whatever Jesus tells them"....Work your way through the crowded room....Find the servants and send them to Jesus....Jesus looks startled, maybe a little annoyed. "Fill those jugs with water," he orders....The servers begin filling the jugs....After the jars are filled, Jesus instructs the servant to empty some of the water from the jugs into the pitcher you are holding...."Child, take the pitcher to the head waiter to taste"....Take the full pitcher to the waiter....Be careful, don't spill!....The waiter did not see what happened, so when he tasted the water which Jesus had turned into wine he spoke to you, "This is the finest wine I have ever tasted! You have saved the best for last!"....And so the first miracle that Jesus worked was at Cana in Galilee.

The wedding guests partied until dawn....Then one by one they began the journey to their homes. At last you are alone with Jesus....Look into Jesus' eyes....He is tired but happy ....Mary is very proud of her son....Jesus explains, "My mother, Mary, believed that I could do something about the problem of running out of wine....I wasn't ready to reveal God's glory and power....But, now the time is right. With this sign, I revealed God's glory." Jesus reaches down, taking your hand in his, and makes his way out into the garden....The sweet smell of honeysuckle hangs heavy in the night air...."Come and join me," he says, patting the seat next to his....Jesus settles on a swing near the sweetness of the rose gardens....He lifts you into the security of his lap. This is a good time, a happy time....

The soft voice of Jesus breaks the silence of the evening air ...."What can I do for you, my child?" Jesus whispers.... Settle back in the arms of Jesus and tell him what is on your mind.

I will leave you alone with Jesus for a moment.

Prayer

Jesus, the sign at Cana tells me that you were sent to show God's love. Help me to show people God's love. Help me to remember that when we act in loving ways, things can change, just like the water changed into wine. Amen.

It is time for you to say goodbye to your friend Jesus.... Stand and walk down the path....Open your eyes and return to this room.

Discussion

- Who asked Jesus for help?
- Why did Jesus turn water into wine?
- How do you think the people at the party felt after Jesus did this?
- How do you show love to your friends?

Activity: Plan a Miracle

Ask the students to name one thing they would like to change in the world. Have them name several things and reach a consensus on one particular idea. Discuss various ways the idea can be accomplished.

Jesus Calls Your Name

Scripture: Mt 4:12-23; Mk 1:14-20
Feast: Third Sunday of Ordinary Time (AB)
Music Suggestion: "By Name I Have Called You"/*Gentle Sounds*

Supplies: radio, candle, music tape
Optional: list of the children's names

Bring a radio. Begin by showing the radio.

Can you hear the music? Can you hear all the people talking right now? Probably not, but I have brought something to help us listen. (*Turn on the radio.*) When we turn it on, we can hear the music and the people telling us important news.

The people talking and the music are always there, but of course we must be listening. (*Turn off the radio.*) If we turn it off, we cannot hear the message.

God's Word, the message, is always here, just like the music on the radio, but first we must turn it on, by reading the word, then we must tune in to God. God calls us by name, but if we are not listening we will not be able to hear the call. At the time of Jesus the world didn't have radios and TVs; Jesus needed help in getting his message across. Help came when four fishermen "tuned in to God" as they were casting their nets out to sea.

Let's unzip our imaginations and join the fishermen on the shore of the Sea of Galilee.

Meditation

Close your eyes....Take a deep breath....Whisper "Jesus" as you let your breath out slowly....Get comfortable....Here we go....

You are walking on the sandy beach by the Sea of Galilee ....You are waiting for Jesus....The water slides in across the sand, leaving its wet fingerprints upon the ground.... Waves splash against your legs....Smell the seaweed in the summer wind....The air is fresh and clear....Fishermen prepare their boats to go to sea, loadings nets and bait on the rolling wooden decks....As you walk, wet sand curls around your toes....Step heavily on the sand....Pull your foot away....Like magic, the sand erases the footprint with the next wave of water washing it out to sea....There are some fishermen sitting by their boat, rolling a heavy net.... They have long beards, strong shoulders, and hands rough with callouses....You are able to hear them talking happily as they work.

Look out on the water....A small boat bobs in the water.... The fisherman waves....Looking closer, you recognize the man....It is Jesus!....The little wooden boat rolls up on the shore....Sea water washes away the sand....Jesus steps out of the boat....Run to meet him....Jesus is very happy to see you....He is smiling and calls out your name....Listen to Jesus call your name....He bends low and scoops you up into his arms, holding you gently...."Thank you for coming to meet me," Jesus says, giving you an extra hug....Jesus sets your feet upon the sand....He takes your hand....His hands are smooth and soft, not like those of the fishermen ....Hand in hand, you walk down the beach, the sea water dripping from the hem of Jesus' clothing...."Do you see those fishermen rolling their nets?" he asks...."I have come to see if those men will come with me and be my helpers" ....Jesus then asks you to wait for him....Jesus walks over to the men....They glance up, barely seeming to notice him.... "Peter and Andrew, will you come with me?" Jesus asked ....Their eyes grow large in amazement that Jesus knows their names....Jesus begins to speak to them....Soon, they "tune in" to Jesus' request and, placing their folded nets in the boat, walk toward you with Jesus...."Meet my new friends." You shake the coarse, rough hand of Peter.... Andrew is much younger than his brother....His eyes twinkle with new excitement....You continue walking along the shore with Jesus and his new friends....Jesus points to another small boat where two fishermen are about to set out to sea....Jesus walks quickly now, calling out, "James, John, come follow me, and I will show you a new way of life"....Can you see the surprise on their faces?....They row back into shore....Jesus invites them to join the group.... Putting away their fishing lines, they climb out of the boat and follow Jesus....

You tug on Jesus' sleeves...."Where are we going?" you ask...."I will show you the way. Do not be afraid," Jesus answers....The four fishermen walk happily along, chatting excitedly....You hear James say, "I really don't know why I decided to follow him. I just knew it was right"....Jesus smiles at you, placing his hand on your shoulder....Feel the warmth of his hand....Leaving the others to prepare for their journey across the sea, you and Jesus walk to a small bonfire on the edge of the shore....Settle yourself in the sand....Jesus leans forward, warming his hands by the fire, then takes your hands in his....He questions, "Will you be my helper, too?" Take a moment to talk with Jesus.... *(Pause for half a minute or until the children grow restless.)*

Prayer

Jesus, my Lord, you call me by name to follow you. Help me to follow you more closely each day. May I help others to follow you. Amen.

It is time to leave Jesus....Walk with Jesus where the four men wait in a boat....Tell Jesus goodbye....Wave goodbye to your new friends....Open your eyes and return to this room.

Discussion

- Whom did Jesus ask to be his first helpers?
- How did the fishermen answer Jesus' request?
- How can you show Jesus that you want to be his helper, too?

Prayer Time

1. Lower the lights and light a candle.

2. Ask the children to be very quiet, close their eyes, and unzip their imaginations once again. Say, "Jesus is calling you to follow him. Listen carefully."

3. Read off the children names saying, "(*Name*), will you follow me?" Ask the children to respond with, "Yes, Lord, Yes."

Finding Happiness with Jesus

Scripture: Mt 5:1-12
Feast: Fourth Sunday of Ordinary Time (A)
Music Suggestion: "Peace Is Flowing Like a River"/*Gentle Sounds*

Ask the children, "What makes you happy?" List their answers on the chalkboard or newsprint.

Would you like to be happy forever? Sure you would! Jesus had a great deal to say about how to find happiness. Jesus explains that true happiness comes from God no matter what sadness we might be going through. He also tells us that we cannot find all of our happiness in having fun, in eating all the candy we want, and in being rich. What do you think Jesus means by "real happiness?" One day a large crowd of people ask Jesus the same question. Shall we find out what Jesus had to say? Let's unzip our imaginations, joining the crowd that surrounds Jesus.

Meditation

Close your eyes....Wiggle your toes....Take a deep breath ....Let it out slowly....Whisper "Jesus"....Relax....

It is early morning....The sun has just peeked over the top of the mountain....Your bones feel cold and stiff....You fold your arms tightly across your chest, gathering your blanket about you....Last night your bed was the cold, hard ground ....You have waited all night at the foot of the mountain where Jesus went to pray....You can hear the murmuring and shuffling of restless feet around you....Many people have gathered during the night, hoping to see and hear Jesus....Some have come expecting miracles....

The clouds slowly float into nothingness, no longer covering the warmth of the sun....You stretch your arms and legs like a lazy cat in the sunshine of your garden....Today will be a good day....The crowd begins moving up the steep hillside ....People are excited about seeing Jesus....The murmuring now turns into excited shouts of "Jesus is coming! Jesus is here!"....The crowd surrounds Jesus, everyone trying to touch him....It is said that if you are able to touch Jesus you will be cured of your sickness....There are many miracles this morning....

Jesus now moves back up the hill, above the crowd, so that everyone can see him....Can you see him? (*Pause for several seconds.*)....The wind blows Jesus' long, dark hair....He reaches to pull his hair from his face....A baby lamb curls up at his feet....Puppies and kittens of all sizes and colors romp and play in the tall grass....Jesus stops to pet a black puppy's long, curly-haired ears....He laughs as the puppy's wet tongue licks his cheeks....You feel happiness start at your toes and rise to your head....This is a good day!

Someone in the crowd calls out, "Jesus, tell us how to find happiness"....You wonder how anyone could want more happiness than you feel at this moment....Jesus, standing tall on the hillside, begins to speak. "You are a very happy person if you know the joy of just being alive. All the money in the world cannot buy the best things in life"....The crowd oohs and ahhhs, nodding their heads in understanding.... You begin to push your way through the tangle of long legs

and nervous feet....You want to be close to Jesus....Jesus
notices you working your way through the throng of people
....Jesus motions for you to come and sit at his feet....Take
a seat on the dew-covered grass....A lamb nuzzles your
pocket for goodies....Jesus places a finger over his lips....It
is time to be quiet....

Jesus speaks again, "You are a happy person if you know
how to be kind and understanding. People will want to be
your friend"....Jesus bends now, whispering in your ear,
"Are you always kind to everyone, especially your brother
or sister?" I will give you time to answer Jesus in your heart.
(*Pause.*) Jesus pats you on the shoulder, continuing to
speak to the people...."You are a happy person if you
always try to make the world a better place to live." Jesus
leans forward, asking you, "Do you always share with
others? Are you able to give without thinking about what
you will get back?" (*Pause briefly.*)

"You are a happy person if God is number one in your life.
You are a happy person if you work to have true peace
throughout the world." Jesus pauses, putting his arm
around you, and whispers, "Peace begins in your heart and
in your own home. Do you spread my peace at home?"
Answer Jesus in your heart. (*Pause.*)

"You are a happy person if you can stand up for what you
believe in. People will respect you"....Jesus walks to a patch
of blooming flowers. Stooping over, he takes a beautiful
butterfly upon his long finger and then continues...."You
are a happy person if you don't let it bother you when
people pick on you and call you names because you believe
in me. Be happy about that because you will have a great
reward in heaven." Jesus raises his arm high above his
head, releasing the butterfly to sail with the breeze. "If you
do these things you shall truly be a child of God, and you
will find all the happiness that your heart can hold." Jesus
slowly turns from the people, signaling a time to close....

Jesus turns his back to the throng of people. Bending low on one knee, he places his hands on your head....You can feel the touch of his hands on top of your head....He looks deep into your eyes and says, "You are a child of God....I love you." I will leave you with Jesus for a moment....Speak with your heart.

Prayer

Jesus, I love you. Help me to remember that true happiness comes in knowing you. May I follow in your footsteps to reach out to others. Amen.

It is time for Jesus to continue his journey....Say goodbye to your friend, Jesus....Wave goodbye to your friends on the hillside....Open your eyes and return to our room....

Discussion

- How do Jesus' instructions on finding happiness compare with our first list? How are they different? How are they the same?
- What did Jesus mean, "Peace begins in your heart and in your own home?" How can we see that this happens?
- Jesus wants us to trust in God in times of sadness and difficulty. He tells us that if we trust in him, nothing can take our happiness away from us. How can we show that we trust God?

Activity

1. Go over the beatitudes covered in the meditation, making sure the children understand what Jesus is asking them to do.

2. Divide into two or three groups. Assign a beatitude to each group, asking them to discuss what it means to them and then act out an example situation. Be ready

with some clues or ideas, but allow the children to be creative.

Prayer Time

LEADER: Let us give thanks for being a child of God and pray that everyone will know the happiness of God.

Join in a circle, holding hands. Pray the Lord's Prayer.

Standing Up for What Is Right

Scripture: Lk 4:21-30
Feast: Fourth Sunday of Ordinary Time (C)
Music Suggestion: "Pardon Your People"/*Gentle Sounds*

Has anyone moved from one neighborhood into a new one? Did you ever go back and visit your old friends? Were they friendly? Was everything just like you left it? Probably not. Nothing ever stays the same. Do you think Jesus ever had that problem? Would the people from his old neighborhood welcome Jesus? The answer to this question may surprise you. Let's unzip our imaginations to be with Jesus when he returns to his boyhood home.

Meditation

Close your eyes....Wiggle your toes....Take a deep breath ....Let it out slowly....Whisper "Jesus"....Relax....

You are in the synagogue in Jesus' home town, Nazareth.... Sit on a cushion near the feet of Jesus....The people chatter among themselves, "We have never had anyone this important come to Nazareth before," the man in the front row says proudly....The people are flattered that someone so important came from their home town....Jesus slowly stands, taking the place of honor....Jesus begins to read the

112

text, "The Spirit of the Lord is on me, because he has anointed me to preach good news to the poor"....Jesus rolls up the scroll and hands it to you....Jesus continues, "These scriptures came true today!"....The crowd moves forward, muttering to themselves, "Isn't he Joseph's son?" "You speak in riddles!" shouts another. "He is only the carpenter's son!"...."God has not anointed this simple man," barks a man from the back of the room....The crowd grows restless and angry....

Jesus sees the look on your face....He lays his reassuring hand on your head...."Show us a miracle!"...."We came for the miracles. Stop this ridiculous talk!" shouts another.... The crowd grows angry....You are afraid for Jesus, but he continues to speak God's words....Suddenly, the people stand, raising their fists in anger....The people push forward, grabbing Jesus and tossing him out the door of the synagogue....A large man throws Jesus to the ground.... You hide beneath the branches of an olive tree. The people mob Jesus, taking him to the edge of a hill to push him over the cliff...."Run, Jesus, run," you whisper to yourself.... Jesus calmly looks at the crowd, walking through their midst as though they did not exist.... Jesus calls his disciples to follow...."Hurry, Child," he calls to you....Jesus slips out of sight of the people who want to kill him....Jesus stops now on the roadway, waiting for you to catch up....

On the way to Capernaum he slows his pace, knowing that you are very tired...."Jesus, you could have told the people what they wanted to hear. You could have performed a miracle....Why didn't you?" you ask....Jesus studies the question for a few moments, then answers, "I chose to speak out for God. You, too, are called to speak in my name. Did you know that a call from God can be a simple tugging on your heart or a nudge to choose the right action?"....Jesus places his arm around your shoulders, "I know that it is not always easy to be laughed at when you confront someone because of how they act, or if you see someone stealing, but this is what I ask you to do."

Jesus stops to lift you on a small rock wall surrounding the town of Capernaum....Jesus looks deep within your eyes....It feels as though he can see through you, then speaks, "Close your eyes for a minute and think of a time when you stood up for a friend in trouble or when a friend stood by your side when you were in need." (*Pause.*) "Will you stand by me?" Jesus asks.

I will leave you alone to answer Jesus. Listen carefully to what he tells you.

Prayer
Jesus, may I come to know the joy of standing by those I love. Give me the courage I need to always speak out for what is right. I ask this in your name. Amen.

It is time to leave....Give Jesus a hug....Turn and walk away ....Stop and wave goodbye....Open your eyes and return to this room.

Discussion

- What can we do in our class to make a better world?
- Why do you think the people of Jesus' home town did not accept him?
- Do you think that people always want to hear the truth? What keeps Jesus from doing all he would like to do for us? (*Our lack of faith*)

Jesus Takes Charge

Scripture: Mt 8:23-27; Mk 4:35-42; Lk 8:22-25
Feast: Twelfth Sunday of Ordinary Time (B)
Music Suggestion: "Song over the Water"/*Instruments of Peace*
 OR "When You Seek Me"/*Gentle Sounds*

Have you ever felt a wind blow so strongly with rain that
you thought the whole sky opened up? Have you ever seen
the wind bend trees? Sometimes the wind pushes you down
the street. That is really scary! What do you do when you
are afraid? It is always good to go to someone that you
really trust, isn't it? One time the apostles found themselves
in a terrible wind storm on the Sea of Galilee. Let's unzip
our imaginations and see what happened when the apostles
were frightened.

Meditation

Close your eyes....Shrug your shoulders....Take a deep
breath....Let it out slowly....Whisper "Jesus"....Relax....

You are sitting on the sandy shore of the Sea of Galilee,
waiting for Jesus....Water pushes into shore, then rushes
back into the sea, leaving damp fingerprints on the shore
....Several small boats prepare to cast off....Fishing nets and
fishing poles are piled high....Peter loads baskets of food on
the deck of his boat....Throwing fishing poles in for good
measure, Peter calls out, "Ready to go"....John jumps on

the rocking deck, then leans over the side, offering you his hand....Jesus is the last one to board....He takes his seat quietly, then looks over at you and smiles....He lays his head back on the seat of the boat....Take a deep breath of the sea air....It smells fresh and clean....A cool breeze blows your hair about your face....Feel the gentle rolling of waves against the bottom of the boat....You feel comfortable and safe....Jesus is fast asleep, his head resting on a cushion.... Take off your jacket and cover the sleeping Jesus....Peter speaks in a loud whisper, telling everyone, "Don't wake Jesus"....A hush falls over the boat....All is quiet except for the sound of the waves....

Suddenly, the sky grows dark....Clouds cover the last rays of the sun....Hold out your hand....You can barely see your own hand....The winds begin to blow, tossing the boat like a small toy in the bathtub....Hang on to the railing....Here comes another wave....Cold sea water washes into the boat....Wind pushes the wooden boat into the air, then pulls it into the hard, dark wetness of the sea....Peter, water dripping from his beard, holds tightly to the wheel....He looks worried....John and James pull the rope on the sails ....James falls to the deck with the force of the wind and rain....Are you afraid?....The apostles cling to the railings and to each other....The winds howl....Cover your ears.... Peter calls out, "Wake up Jesus!"....Jesus sleeps on....

Andrew, his hands shaking with fright, comes to your side...."Crawl into the back of the boat, child, and wake Jesus"....The boat is filling with water....Make your way over the seats, past James and John....Place your hand on Jesus....Wake him....Andrew cries, "We are going to drown!"....

Jesus wakes up....The winds pulls at his hair....He looks down at his feet now covered with sea water....He glances around the bouncing boat....Turn to Jesus and ask for his help....He is very gentle....Patting you on the shoulder,

Jesus stands with his legs braced, swaying from side to side....He slowly raises his hands over the battling sea and commands, "Peace! Be stilled!"....The wind stops!....The sea is once again calm....You feel the warmth of the sun.... Jesus pulls you close to his side, looks at his confused disciples and questions, "Why are you afraid? Don't you believe in me?"

Peter, rubbing his chin whiskers, asks, "Who are you, Jesus, that even the wind and the sea obey you?"....Peter shakes his head and looks out at the calm sea....

Jesus takes your hands, and looks into your eyes, "It is all right to feel afraid. I hope that you always come to me when you are afraid and lonely. I will always be here for you. Do you trust me? Do you believe in me?" Jesus whispers....

I will leave you alone so that you may talk to Jesus. If you have any fears that have been bothering you, talk to your friend Jesus about them.

Prayer
Jesus, thank you for calming the storm. Thank you, Lord, for your loving protection. Help me through the "storms" or problems in my life. Help me to always place my trust in you. Amen.

The boat pulls into the shore....It is time to tell Jesus goodbye....Step out of the boat....Turn and walk away.... Return to this room....

Discussion
- What did Jesus say to the Sea of Galilee?
- What did Jesus ask the disciples?
- What do you do when you are afraid?

Jesus Tells Us a Story

Scripture: Mt 13:1-23
Feast: Fifteenth Sunday of Ordinary Time (A)
Music Suggestion: "Gather Us In"/*Instruments of Peace*

Have you ever planted seeds? What happened after you planted the seeds? Did you poke the seeds down into the soil, or did you just lay the seeds upon the top of the soil? It makes a difference how you plant the seeds, doesn't it?

Jesus tells us a story about a child, near your age, that was given some seeds to plant. Jesus told a lot of little stories. In the story that we are about to hear, Jesus was really talking about a message of love. Let's unzip our imaginations and listen to Jesus tell his story.

Meditation

Close your eyes....Shrug your shoulders....Take a deep breath....Let it out slowly....Whisper "Jesus" softly.... Relax....

Picture Jesus walking out the front door of your house....He walks down the path to the street....Run after Jesus....Jesus motions for you to hurry...."You need to walk a little faster if you are going with me," he says laughing....Jesus takes hold of your hand....You look up into his smiling face....

Everything seems just right!....In the distance you see the
blue-green waters of the lake....

You and Jesus, walking hand in hand, make your way down
the grassy slope....Tall grass tickles your legs.... Ripples of
water wash across the shore....Smell the fresh air....Jesus
sits down by the shore, removing his sandals....He wiggles
his toes in the cool waters....You pull your shoes off and dip
your feet into the water.... Jesus is laughing....He splashes
cold droplets of water on your face...."Would you like to
hear a story?" he asks....

Jesus begins telling you stories about God....Soon, a crowd
of people gather to hear his stories....A group of little
children play nearby....People are shoving and pushing,
trying to get a glimpse of Jesus....Jesus is standing....He
moves to a high rock....Still the people push forward....
Jesus walks toward his little wooden boat and motions for
you to untie the rope hitched to a tree....Hop into the boat
with Jesus....Pull up on the large rock anchor....Jesus
begins rowing out a few feet on the lake so that all the
people can see and hear him....Water laps on the side of
the boat....Jesus stops rowing....He stands in the rocking
boat....The crowd now lines the water's edge....Jesus begins
to tell this story....

"A child planted some seeds one day. As he scattered the
seeds across the ground, the seeds began to roll about.
Some fell beside a path, and birds quickly came and carried
them off. Some fell on rocky soil, but the hot sun soon
scorched them and they withered and died. Other seeds fells
among the thorns, and the thorns choked the plant. But
some seeds fell on good soil and grew tall and strong! The
child was able to pick all the vegetables that the family could
use with plenty left for the neighbors."

The crowd likes Jesus' story, but some of them do not
understand what he is talking about....They are scratching

their heads and talking among themselves....You too wonder what he was talking about!....Jesus smiles at you, knowing that you are confused....Taking his seat in the boat, he begins to row toward the opposite shore....Drag your arm in the water....Feel the cool spray splashing against the boat....Jesus pulls into shore and steps out....He takes your hand, leading you to a campfire....Several of Jesus' disciples are warming themselves by the sparking fire....They greet Jesus and you....His friends tell Jesus that even they didn't understand his story....

Jesus squats down near the fire....Looking up into your eyes, he asks, "Don't you know that I wasn't talking about a vegetable garden? I was talking about people who hear my message of love. The hard path where some seeds fell is like the heart of a person who hears the Good News but doesn't understand it. The rocky soil represents the heart of a person who hears the Good News and is happy but then soon forgets about God. The seeds among the thorns are like God's words growing in a person's heart but get choked out, and the person does less and less for God." "How about the seeds on the good soil?" James the disciple asks....Jesus rises, holding his hands over the warmth of the fire...."Those who listen to the Good News and accept and understand my message grow in love and spread it to other people. People who hear my message of love but don't accept it wither away on the branch and have nothing to give to others....Listen to my message, understand what I mean, and then spread the Good News to others."

The disciples wander off to walk along the shore....You are alone with Jesus....Sparks from the campfire scatter into the cool fall day....Jesus moves over on the log, inviting you to sit beside him....You are all alone with Jesus....All you can hear is the crackling fire and the voice of Jesus....I will leave you here to talk to Jesus in the quiet of your heart....

Prayer

Jesus, help me to grow in your love. May I have your strength to share your Good News with others. Thank you for being my friend. Amen.

It is time for you to leave now....Tell Jesus goodbye....Turn and walk away....Start up the grassy hillside....Open you eyes and return to this room.

Discussion

- What happens to the seed on good soil?
- How can we be good soil?
- Who is the child in Jesus' story?
- What happens to the seed thrown on the path? How does this happen? (*Not paying attention or understanding what you hear.*)

Love Your Neighbor As Yourself

Scripture: Lk 10:25-37
Feast: Fifteenth Sunday of Ordinary Time (C)
Music Suggestion: "Pardon Your People"/*Gentle Sounds*

Can anyone tell me what the word "neighbor" means? What do you think it means to be a good neighbor? Who is your neighbor? What are some things that you could do to be a good neighbor? Jesus talked about the importance of being a good neighbor. He told us to love our neighbors as much as we love ourselves. Jesus taught us that we were to act as good neighbors to everyone.

Jesus wanted us to understand that we are neighbors to everyone in the world. He wanted us to always be willing to share God's love with others, regardless of where they come from or what color their skin is. One day Jesus told a story about what it means to be a good neighbor. Why don't we join Jesus in the shade of an apple tree and listen as he tells the story?

Meditation

Close your eyes....Take a deep breath....Let it out slowly.... Whisper "Jesus"....

Smell the sweet, sweet fragrance of apple blossoms....Look at the tree....Pink petals slowly fall to the ground....A carpet of green grass covers the hillside....Listen to the soft laughter of children playing....There is Jesus!....He is leaning against the crooked trunk of the tree....Jesus looks at you, smiles, and calls your name....Run to greet Jesus.... The dew on the grass tickles your toes....Jesus folds his arms about you....Take a seat beside Jesus as he begins his story.

"You have asked me to explain what it means to love your neighbor....This little story may help you to understand.... Once upon a time there was a man going from Jerusalem to Jericho. The road from Jerusalem to Jericho was very dangerous for people to travel. Robbers often hid behind the big rocks on either side of the road. And no one ever traveled on the road alone. But the man didn't think about the danger and began his journey alone. The worst happened not far from Jerusalem. Robbers attacked the man, stole all his money, took his clothes, and beat him very badly. The robbers thought that he was dead when they were finished with him.

"A priest was walking down the same road. He saw the poor man lying by the side of the road but just kept walking. The next person came by was a Levite, someone who worked in the temple. He saw the man on the ground but chose to walk around him, closing his ears to the injured man's cries for help. Later, in the afternoon, another man came by. This man was from Samaria. Now remember, Jews were not supposed to even talk to anyone from Samaria. The Jews thought that the Samaritans were bad people and the Samaritans thought the Jews were bad people. But the Samaritan saw the man lying on the ground and felt sorry for him. The Samaritan came up to the poor man. He put bandages on him and washed him as best he could. Then the Samaritan lifted him on his horse and took him to the nearest inn where he put him to bed and took care of him. The next morning the Samaritan gave the innkeeper money to take care of the man. He also told the innkeeper, 'If it costs more than what I am giving you, I will pay the rest when I come back.'"....Jesus sips water from a small clay cup, then asks a question, "Now which of these three men was a good neighbor?"....Everyone listening to the story begins murmuring among themselves. "The one who was kind and took care of him." "The Samaritan showed God's love," calls another voice from the crowd. Jesus nods his head in agreement, "Yes, that's right. Now go and treat others the same way"....

Jesus takes your hand in his....He leans very close and whispers, "It is hard to be a good neighbor when everyone else isn't. It's hard to be a good neighbor when nobody says, 'Thank you for helping me'.... It's hard to be a good neighbor sometimes, isn't it?"

I will leave you alone with Jesus. Take a few minutes to talk this over with Jesus.

Prayer

Dear Jesus, at times I thought I was too busy to help others or that someone else would take care of the problem. I do not always take the time to be a good neighbor to others. I am sorry. Help me to help others, especially those who are ignored or forgotten. Thank you, Jesus, for loving me. Amen.

It is time for you to leave....Give Jesus a hug....Remember his words as you walk away....Open your eyes and return to this room.

Discussion

- What happened to the man who traveled down the road?
- Which one of the three men would you say is the good neighbor?

- Can someone share a time that you acted like the good neighbor?

Activity

1. Invite the children to retell the story, bringing in as many details as possible.

2. Have the children sit together in a group. Pick a panel of six judges. Select children to act the role of the Levite, priest, and Samaritan. Ask the judges to call forth first the priest and then the Levite, asking, "Why didn't you help the man?" The priest and the Levite give their excuses. Children can question their reasons. Next have the Samaritan come forward. The judges ask, "Why did you stop and help?" The Samaritan responds.

3. Conclude by asking all the children: How do you think God wants us to treat each other?

A Treasure Hunt

Scripture: Mt 13:44-52
Feast: Seventeenth Sunday of Ordinary Time (A)
Music Suggestion: "By Name I Have Called You"/*Gentle Sounds*

What would you do if you found a buried treasure? (*List answers on chalkboard or newsprint.*) Would this make you happy? One night while Jesus was together with his friends he told a story about a treasure hunt. Let's unzip our imaginations and listen to Jesus' story.

Meditation

Close your eyes....Wiggle your toes....Take a deep breath ....Let is out slowly....Whisper "Jesus"....Relax....

You are sitting in front of a campfire....Sparks from the fire fly around your head, popping and cracking....If you listen very carefully you can hear the crickets singing their song ....Frogs from the nearby pond croak in the evening air ....Jesus and his disciples are gathered around the fire, enjoying its warmth....Jesus looks up from the fire and calls your name....He pats the ground, inviting you to sit down next to him....Run quickly to his side....It is nice to have Jesus as your special friend, isn't it?...."I am so glad that you are here," he says, patting you on the back....Peter is finishing the last bites of supper....James pokes at the fire with a stick, sending popping sparks into the night air....

126

"Let me tell you a story about a buried treasure, and let's see if you can tell me what the treasure is. Once upon a time, there were two men looking for a treasure....The first man went into a field and began digging holes all over the field....Finally, he found the buried treasure....The young man lifted the treasure from its earth-filled grave, wiping away the dirt and rocks....Then, looking around to make sure that no one saw him, he opened the treasure, peeking inside....It was so wonderful that he could hardly believe his eyes!....The treasure was much too wonderful to keep in his house, so he found a new hiding place. 'What if someone else finds my treasure?' he thought to himself. So the young man went out and sold everything that he owned in the whole world....Then he took the money and bought the field where his treasure was buried. Now he truly owned the treasure.

"The second man was a shopkeeper who sold only the finest pearls. The white-haired man searched the world over for the most perfect pearl....After many years of searching and buying and selling pearls, he found the most perfect pearl of them all. The old man was very happy—but he found that the pearl cost a great deal of money. He went back home and counted all of his coins, but there was only one way he could ever buy the perfect pearl....He sold everything that he owned: his house, his clothes, his jewels, his land....At last, he was able to buy the pearl."

Jesus stands and stretches....Turning to you, he asks, "What is the treasure?"....Answer Jesus....(*Pause briefly*.)....Jesus listens, then explains, "The kingdom of heaven is like the buried treasure and the fine pearl....The two men were willing to give up everything they had in order to make the treasures their own....In order for you to find the treasure, God's kingdom, you must be loving and share what you have with others"....

The disciples gather together, discussing Jesus' lesson....
You are all alone with Jesus, enjoying the warmth of the
fire and the time with Jesus....Take a few moments and talk
with Jesus....Tell him what is on your heart....Jesus lowers
himself down on knee, looks into your eyes, and asks, "Are
you willing to be loving and to share with everyone?"....I
will leave you alone with Jesus to talk this over....(*Pause for
half a minute or until the children are restless.*)

Prayer

Jesus, thank you for telling me this story.
Sometimes it is hard for me to share with others.
Help me to act in loving ways toward my family,
friends, and strangers. Give me strength to follow
your example. Amen.

It is time to say goodbye to Jesus now....Feel his strong
arms around you....Turn away from the campfire....Walk
down the crooked path....Return to this room....

Discussion

- What does the story of the buried treasure and the pearl
  teach you about the value of the kingdom of God?
- What would you be willing to do to be part of the
  kingdom of God?

Enough Is More Than Enough

Scripture: Mt 14:13-21; Jn 6:1-15
Feast: Seventeenth Sunday of Ordinary Time (B)
        Eighteenth Sunday of Ordinary Time (A)
Music Suggestion: "Gather Us In"/Instruments of Peace

How many of you have ever been on a picnic? What did you take to the picnic? Did your mom ever forget to pack the food? It wouldn't be a picnic without the food, would it? Did Jesus ever go on a picnic?

One day Jesus went on an unexpected picnic and he didn't have enough food. The big difference between our picnics and this picnic is that he had more than 5,000 people to feed! Can you imagine how much food he needed to feed that many people? Let's unzip our imaginations and join Jesus and his disciples to see how they handled feeding such a crowd.

Meditation

Close your eyes....Wiggle your toes....Take a deep breath ....Let it out slowly....Whisper "Jesus"....Relax....

You are standing in a grassy meadow....The tall blades of grass sway in the gentle summer breeze....There are wildflowers peeking through tall blades of grass....The blue waters of the Sea of Galilee stretch as far as your eye can see....You are waiting for your friend Jesus to come ashore ....A small wooden boat pulls onto the shore....A saddened Jesus steps out of the boat....Run down the grassy knoll to meet him....Call out to him....Jesus swoops you up into his arms and holds you tight, not saying a word....Tears fall from Jesus' eyes....Wipe away his tears....Hold your hand, moistened with his precious tears, next to your heart.... Jesus has been told that his cousin, John the Baptist, was killed by King Herod....It is hard to lose someone you care about....Take a moment to comfort Jesus....*(Pause briefly.)*

The disciples climb quietly out of the bobbing boat, making their way through the damp sand....They join you and Jesus on the pathway....John, wiping his sand-caked feet, notices the large crowd that has gathered to meet Jesus...."Lord, the people walked for miles around the shore to see you" ....Jesus sighs, takes your hand in his, and begins walking toward the growing crowd....Jesus walks among the people, blessing and healing the sick....A small boy leaning on a wooden crutch, his leg wrapped in bandages, reaches out to touch Jesus....Jesus gently places his hand on the sick child's head, smiles, and then walks away....The boy jumps with joy, tossing his crutch into the brush....You are nearly knocked from your feet by the crush of the crowd....

Stand on your tiptoes....All you can see is a wall of people surrounding Jesus.

The sun is beginning to set behind the hill....Peter pushes his way through the crowd....Breathlessly he tells Jesus, "We have been talking, Lord. It is late in the day....Send the people on their way....We do not have enough food to feed ourselves, let alone this crowd!"...."There is no need to send them away....Gather the food together and feed the people." Jesus walks into the crowd....Peter's mouth drops open....He walks off muttering to himself....Jesus turns to

you, "Help Peter gather the food....Place all that you find
beneath those trees"....Take the empty basket from
Thomas....As you weave through the multitude, you notice
a small child motioning to you....The child hands you his
small basket of bread and dried fish...."This is all that I
have, but you may share this with Jesus," the child tells you
....This small amount is all the food you can find....Reach
into the small knapsack tied around your waist....Pull out
the bread you were saving and place it in the basket....

Join the disciples, placing the gathered food at Jesus'
feet....Count the loaves of bread, "One, two, three, four,
five loaves of bread and two fish is all that we have. This will
never be enough," Peter cautions Jesus. "Invite the people
to spread blankets on the grass and prepare to share a
meal," Jesus orders....Jesus raises the food above his head,
offering God a prayer of thanksgiving....He hands the bread
to Timothy, "Pass this out to the people"....Timothy breaks
off hunks of bread, passing it to waiting hands....Jesus turns
to you, handing you a fish...."Share this with our friends,
child"....Walk among the sea of faces....Break off pieces of
the fish....Share them with the grateful people....When the
last person is fed, join Jesus, who is sitting beneath the
golden-yellow trees....Jesus shares his food with you,
breaking the bread and fish into pieces....Jesus smiles,
"When I have a picnic, I really have a picnic, don't I?"....
You and Jesus share the meal and laughter....

"Gather the leftovers and bring them to me," Jesus tells the
disciples....Grab an empty basket....Return to Jesus with the
gathered leftovers....The disciples place their overflowing
baskets next to yours....There are twelve baskets of bread
and fish left over!....Jesus notices the look of disbelief on
your face....

"Come here, my child," Jesus says, patting the ground next
to him...."Why are you surprised that we have leftovers?....
God always gives us more than we can use....There is more

sunshine than we can ever see....Look at the grass covering this meadow....We cannot count the blades of grass.... There are more roaring rivers and babbling brooks than we can ever hear....You have more clothes than you can wear at one time....God is good to us, so do not be surprised that we have enough food to eat....When God gives us anything, he makes sure we have enough, and leftovers."

Jesus stands, stretches out his arms as far as possible, and says, "God loves you this much." Jesus smiles down at you ....Taking your hand in his, he looks into your eyes...."Are you willing to share God's love and blessings with others?" ....I will give you quiet time so that you can talk to Jesus....

Prayer
Jesus, I don't stop to think about how many blessings I have. Instead, I complain, always wanting more. Help me to share God's love and blessing with others. I love you. Amen.

It is time to leave Jesus and the picnic behind....Say goodbye....Reach into your knapsack, give Jesus something that you brought with you from home, something that you treasure. (*Pause briefly.*) Get up and walk away through the field of grass....Open your eyes and return to this room....

Discussion

- Would anyone like to share thoughts about Jesus' picnic? What happened? Were you surprised?
- Did the disciples trust Jesus that five loaves and two fish would feed all the people?
- How did you feel when Jesus told you to divide the food and feed the people? Is there anything other than food that you are able to share?
- What would you have brought from home to give to Jesus? (*Something you treasure*)

31   Jesus and Peter Take a Walk on the Water

Do Not Be Afraid

Scripture: Mt 14:22-33
Feast: Nineteenth Sunday of Ordinary Time (A)
Music Suggestion: "Sea of Change"/*Ceremony*
      OR "Song over the Water"/*Instruments of Peace*

How many of you have ever gone on a boat ride? Would
you be afraid if you were in the middle of the sea when a
storm came and tossed the boat from side to side? Would
you be willing to try walking on the water if someone you
trusted said you could? It is not always easy to trust that
much, is it? Peter was in a boat one time and Jesus told him
to walk on the water. Let's close our eyes and unzip our
imaginations now and see how Peter responded to Jesus.

Meditation

Close your eyes....Shrug your shoulders....Forget about all
the noises in the room....Take a deep breath....Let it out
slowly....Whisper "Jesus"....Relax....

You are sitting beside a lake....The day has just turned to
evening....Waters from the lake lap at the shore....Take a
deep breath....Smell the cool fresh air....There are a few
boats on the calm waters....Fishermen return to shore....
Look down the shoreline....Jesus and his disciples are
stepping into a small fishing boat....Call out to Jesus....
Looking up, Jesus recognizes you...."Would you like to

come with us?" he asks....Run down to the water's edge....
Wet sand seeps up through your toes, Quish-Quash, as you
run....

Jesus looks very tired but he is smiling at you...."Help Peter
push out into the water," he tells you....Peter's red scraggly
beard outlines his weathered face...."Push as hard as you
can," Peter tells you....At last the boat frees itself from the
sandy beach....Hop on board....Your foot drags through the
cool water....The soft breeze of evening blows through your
hair....Jesus moves over, making room for you to join him
...."Row the boat to the opposite side of the lake," he tells
the men....Moonlight streams across the water, lighting the
way....When at last you reach the other shore, a large
mountain rises above the water....Jesus announces that he
is going to climb the mountain and pray to his Father....
Stepping out of the boat, he waves goodbye, instructing the
disciples to come back later.

As the boat leaves the shore and Jesus behind, you feel the
gentle rolling of the waves beneath the boat....Lay your head
down and rest....Hear the soft murmuring of the disciples'
voices; it is time to return to the shore for Jesus....In the
yellow glow of the moonlight the mountain's shadow grows
smaller....The air suddenly stirs around you, blowing your
hair....Water sprays across your face....A sudden windstorm
propels the small boat across the water, The boat bobs like a
rubber duck on the foamy sea....Look around you....James'
hands grip the oars, his knuckles white....The sleeping
disciples are tossed about in the bottom of the boat like rag
dolls....Peter shouts, "The winds are pushing us further out!....
We can't go back and get Jesus"....All the disciples are awake
now, pulling on the oars, but the little boat does not make any
headway....

In the direction of the distant shore a strange figure appears
above the lake....It moves slowly, on top of the water,
toward the boat...."It's a ghost!" the disciples cry....A shiver

goes down your spine...."Let me out of here!" one of the
disciples cries....You peek over the railing of the boat, afraid
to see and afraid not to see the strange happenings...."How
can this be?" you ask....From the shifting waters and fog-
shrouded lake you hear, "Do not be afraid! It is I, Jesus"....
Peer into the fog....The voice sounds like Jesus....It is Jesus!
....He is walking toward you, on the crest of the waves!....
"Who is this?" cry the disciples....Peter stands on the bow
of the boat, his hair pulled back by the force of the wind,
calling out, "If that is you, Lord, tell me to come to you on
the water."

The soft voice of Jesus calls through the damp night air,
"Peter, come to me." Peter hesitates, looking at the other
disciples, then climbs out of the boat, stepping onto the
cold, dark waters....Waves and wind pound the boat....Peter
begins to sink....Winds howl.... "I am afraid! Help me,
Lord!" Peter cries....Jesus reaches out his hand to Peter,
"Oh, you of little faith....Why did you doubt me?" Jesus
calls out....Jesus holds Peter's hand in his, walking toward
the boat.... Suddenly, Jesus stops and calls your name....
"Come to me, my child"....Jesus holds out his arms....The
waves buffet the boat....I will leave you alone to decide if
you are going to step out of the boat onto the water....
(*Pause.*) Tell Jesus how you feel....

When Jesus and Peter climb back into the boat, the wind
stops....The waters are stilled....There is silence everywhere
....You only hear the beating of your own heart....The
disciples fall on their knees...."Truly, you are the Son of
God!"...."May God's blessing be with you of faith," he tells
them....

Jesus settles back against the bow of the boat....Rest your
head against his chest....Listen to Jesus' heart....Place your
hand on your own heart....Feel the rhythm; the two hearts
beat as one....I will leave you alone with Jesus. Share your
thoughts, worries, or problems with him. Jesus loves you....

Prayer

Jesus, I don't always understand what it means to have faith. Sometimes I am afraid and I don't know why. I don't always know who to turn to or what to do. Help me to grow in faith and love. Amen.

It is time to return to shore and say goodbye to Jesus....Step out of the boat....Walk up the sandy path....Turn and wave to your friends....Come back into this room....

Discussion

- Would anyone like to share their experience in the rocking boat?
- If you were Peter, how would you have responded if Jesus invited you to "Come"?
- If Jesus knew that Peter was going to sink, why did he invite him to "Come"?

Invitation to a Special Dinner

Scripture: Lk 14:1,7-14
Feast: Twenty-Second Sunday in Ordinary Time (C)
Music Suggestion: "When You Seek Me"/*Gentle Sounds*

Let's pretend that today is your birthday and you are going to have a big party. Whom would you invite to your party? Do you want someone who will give you a big present? Someone who invited you to his or her party? Someone who will bring something good to eat? Who are you thinking about if you invite someone who will bring a big present? (*Yourself*) Who are you thinking about if you invite someone who will bring something good to eat? Whom do you think Jesus invites to his parties? (*Allow for a variety of answers and include the poor, the sick, the lonely, the sinner.*)

One day Jesus was invited to a dinner party. When he got there he noticed how everyone was trying to sit in the best places at the table. So he told them a story. Let's unzip our imaginations, joining Jesus in the dining room of a mansion.

Meditation

Close your eyes....Wiggle your toes....Take a deep breath ....Let it out slowly....Whisper "Jesus"....Relax....

Waiters scurry about the room with huge trays of food....
Smell the roast turkey, the gravy, the potatoes....It's just like
Thanksgiving at home....The table nearly groans with all the
food....Take your seat at the table....Jesus smiles and
welcomes you to the party....Jesus stands, looking at all the
guests pushing and shoving to sit next to him....Then he
speaks, "Once upon a time a king threw a big party for his
son's birthday. The prince was going to be nine years old.
His father told him that he could invite anyone he wanted to
his birthday party. The prince said to himself, 'I want lots of
presents, so I better invite a lot of people. Prince Andrew's
and Prince Charles' parents are rich, so I bet they will bring
me a good present. I will invite them for sure.'

"The prince thought things over. He remembered that
Brian invited him to a party last year, so he invited Brian.
The prince wanted to go on a trip with Ramon's parents
next month, so the prince said, 'I better invite Ramon or
Ramon may not invite me on the trip.'

"The prince did not invite Kirk because Kirk had a brace on
his arm and could not play ball very well. The prince did not
invite Paul because Paul's parents were very poor and could
not afford to buy him a present. The prince did not invite
Roberto because Roberto never asked him to his party"....
The room grows silent as Jesus walks to the last seat in the
room, the one next to you....As Jesus takes his seat he
asks, "Who was the prince thinking about when he made
out his guest list?"....Jesus continues, "The next time you
have a party, ask some people who probably never get out
to a really nice party. Ask some people who can't invite you
to their party because they may not be able to afford to buy
a cake. If you do this, you will surely be rewarded for being
so kind"....The dinner guests lower their heads sheepishly,
ashamed for the way they have acted....The host quickly
orders the servants to form a big circle with the tables, that
way no one has a better seat than anyone else....The food
is passed and the party begins....

Following the meal, Jesus asks you to join him in the courtyard....The sweet smell of roses and lilacs fills the night air....Jesus sits down on the porch swing, inviting you to join him...."I want you to remember my story. God does not have favorite people. God's circle of love is offered to everyone"....The moonlight casts shadows across the fragrant gardens....Jesus cuddles you beneath his arm, then asks, "What would you tell the prince to do?" (*Pause.*) "Do you ever think that you are better than someone else?"

I will leave you alone to talk with Jesus. Answer his questions with your heart.

Prayer

Jesus, forgive me for the times I think only of my own importance. Let me live as you did, humbly serving God, treating others with love and respect. Help me count all other people as no less important or more important than myself. Thank you for reminding me that I am God's child. Amen.

It is time to leave....Tell Jesus goodbye....Turn and walk through the garden gate....Open your eyes and return to this room.

Discussion

- Whom would Jesus want you to invite to your party?
- Whom would Jesus want you to notice?
- How would you change the ending of Jesus' story?
- What would you tell the prince to do?

Activity

1. Ask the children to form a circle, holding hands. Then ask the children wearing red to step outside the circle. Re-form the circle without them. Next ask the children in

the smaller circle: Would God want the people wearing red to be a part of the circle?

2. Have the children wearing red rejoin the circle and then select another group to step away. Suggestions: those with blue eyes, those wearing black shoes, those who play soccer.

3. Close by asking the children to pray for people God considers important.

> LEADER: Loving God, you love all of us. Each one of us is special. For (*Name*), let us pray to the Lord.
>
> CHILDREN: Lord, hear our prayer.

Ephatha! Be Opened!

Scripture: Mk 7:31-37
Feast: Twenty-Third Sunday of Ordinary Time (B)
Music Suggestion: "Healer of Our Every Ill"/*Instruments of Peace*

Do you know anyone who is deaf? Cover your ears with
your hands. I am going to say something very softly.
"Ephatha! Be opened." Did anyone hear what I said? There
are many people who are deaf, including many children.
Being deaf would be very difficult wouldn't it? What can you
do if you are deaf? Get a hearing aid, read lips, not talk to
anyone? Jesus dealt with the problem in a different manner.
Let's unzip our imaginations and see what Jesus did when a
deaf man asked him for help.

Meditation

Close your eyes....Wiggle your toes one more time....Take
a deep breath....Whisper "Jesus"....Relax....

You have walked many miles across the hot desert sands
today....Dirt is caked on your feet....Sit down by the side of
the road....Take off your shoes....Wipe the dirt away....
Many people travel this road: the old and bent, the young,
the ill, and the lame. They are all following Jesus. People
from town have heard that Jesus has arrived at a small town
near the Sea of Galilee....Look over your shoulder....Below
the hillside the waters of the Sea of Galilee lap against the

shore....Make your way to the water's edge....Dip your feet in the cool waters....You feel the touch of a hand upon your shoulder....Look up....It is your friend Jesus....He smiles broadly, leaning on your shoulder for support....He removes his sandals....Sitting on the shore, Jesus dips his feet in the cooling water....Smiling, and with a twinkle in his eye, he playfully splashes water on you....Take your foot and splash the cool, blue water on Jesus....Jesus looks to the hillside behind him....Many people are gathered...."Come, my child, it is time to for me to return to the people....Dry your feet off," Jesus says, handing you a small towel....Walk hand in hand up the sloping hillside to the waiting mass of people....

Wait for Jesus in the shade of a large rosebush....One by one, he patiently speaks with the people, blessing each one, showing his Father's love and kindness....A small group of people break through the crowd, shouting, "Jesus, Jesus, help this poor man"....At first Jesus does not notice the group....Peter urges the crowd to let the small group of people through....There are four men and two women, all calling Jesus' name, begging for his attention....The woman dressed in a dark blue veil pushes a sad looking little man toward Jesus....The little man trembles at the sight of Jesus, falling upon his knees...."Help him, Jesus. He cannot hear a word, and he speaks very little....He has been this way since birth"...."You are his last hope. Help him, Jesus," begs another....Jesus looks with pity on this poor soul, and a tear falls upon Jesus's cheek....He looks at the crowd crying out for his healing touch....Jesus takes the deaf man's hand and leads him to where you are sitting, away from the crowd.

Jesus places his hand on the frail little man's ears, then he places his fingers on his own tongue and touches the deaf man's ears....Jesus looks up to heaven and with a deep sigh, he says, "Ephatha!" which means "Be Opened!"....
The man's eyes fill with tears of joy....He turns his head to

142

the right and to the left, listening to the sounds of life for
the first time....Turning to the crowd, he shouts, "I can
hear!"....He kisses the hand of Jesus, "Thank you, Lord,
you truly are the Son of God"....The little man grabs your
hands in his, inviting you to join him in a dance of
thanksgiving....Round and round you go....Jesus laughs,
joining the two of you in a circle dance....The crowds cheer
the name of Jesus...."Thank you, Jesus," shouts the
crowd....The crowd gathers around the happy man, lifting
him to their shoulders; they walk toward their homes in the
nearby village....

Jesus looks tired but happy. "Let's rest for a while, child,"
he tells you. You and Jesus walk back to the seaside....It is
almost evening....The sun begins to fall beyond the wall of
the sea....Jesus dabbles his feet in the cool water...."What
can I do for you, my child?" he asks....Take a minute and
think about the times your ears have been closed to the
words of Jesus. Think about some special things you would
like to speak to Jesus about. Perhaps it was when you were
very angry or a time you could have done something for
someone else and failed to do it.

I will leave you alone with Jesus for a few moments.

Prayer

*Jesus, my ears close to you when I become very
angry. My ears close to you when I have the
opportunity to do something for someone else and
fail to do it. Open my ears that I may hear. Move
within my heart that I may love others. Bless my
lips that I may speak your words. Amen.*

It is time to say goodbye to Jesus now....Get up and walk
away....Turn and wave goodbye....Open your eyes and
return to this room.

Discussion

- What do you think the deaf man heard first? What were his first words spoken? What do you think the cured man did with the rest of his life?
- What was the reaction of the crowd?

Activity

Invite the children to act out the story, perhaps having them taking turns being the deaf man.

How Many Times?

Scripture: Mt 18:21-35
Feast: Twenty-Fourth Sunday of Ordinary Time (A)
Music Suggestion: "Pardon Your People"/*Gentle Sounds*

Sometimes it is hard to forgive, isn't it? How do you feel when someone does something really mean to you? Do you always want to forgive? When you have an argument with a brother or sister, what does your mom or dad usually tell you?

One day, Peter asked Jesus how often he must forgive someone. Peter probably thought he was being very generous when he suggested that seven times would be enough. Jesus answered Peter by telling a story. Jesus would like you to hear the story also because he knows how difficult it is to always forgive.

Meditation

Close your eyes....Roll your head from side to side....Take a deep breath....Let it out slowly....Whisper "Jesus"....Relax....

You are in the dining room of a small house....Jesus sits at the head of the table....Candles dismiss their flickering light to dance across the small room....Peter sits on Jesus' right, slowly running his fingers through his red beard....You are seated on the left side of Jesus....He passes you a basket of red grapes....Take a few....Put them in your mouth....Taste the sweetness of the grapes....Jesus smiles, popping a grape into his mouth....You start to say something to Jesus, but Peter interrupts, asking, "Lord, how many times do I forgive someone who has done something that hurts me?" ....Peter smugly leans back on his chair suggesting, "Up to seven times?"....Jesus shakes his head, "Not seven times, but seventy times seven times"....You try to count seventy times seven....Seven times two is fourteen....Seven times seventy is 4,900 times!....Jesus nods his head, "Let me tell you a story that will explain what I mean."

You settle back on one elbow, propping a pillow behind your back....Jesus leans forward, "The kingdom of heaven is like a king who wanted to settle his accounts with his servants. The first servant owed the king millions of dollars. The king was very upset to find out that the servant had no way of paying him, so the king ordered that he and his wife and his children and all that he had be sold to repay the debt. The servant fell on his knees, begging, 'Give me another chance, I will pay back all that I owe you.' The king, feeling sorry for the servant, told him, "I will forget that you owe me this money. Go on your way." The servant ran out the door and down the road, rejoicing. But on the road the servant met one of his fellow servants, who owed him a few dollars. He grabbed him by the neck and began to choke him. 'Pay back what you owe me!' the servant demanded. 'Be patient with me. I will pay back all that I owe,' the man begged. But the first servant refused. Instead he went off and had the man thrown into prison until he could pay the debt. When the other servants saw what had happened, they were very upset and went to the king and told him what had happened. The king called the servant in. 'You are wicked,' he told the servant, 'I forgave your debt because you begged me to. Shouldn't you have mercy on your fellow servant just as I had on you?' The king was very angry and turned the servant over to the jailers to be tortured until he could pay back all he owed"....Jesus rests his elbows on the wooden table. Speaking in a low but firm voice, he continues, "This is how my heavenly Father will treat each one of you unless you forgive your brother from your heart"....

Jesus hugs you and asks, "Do you understand that you are always forgiven by God, but you must in turn always be ready to forgive?....You can never out-forgive God"....The disciples have left the table....You hear a low murmur of voices from the other room....You and Jesus are all alone ...."Perhaps there is someone that you want to forgive," Jesus asks lovingly...."A brother, a sister, a friend"....

I will give you time to talk with Jesus. (*Pause for half a minute or until the children become restless.*)

Prayer

Dear Jesus, sometimes I become very angry and I forget to forgive others. Help me to remember to pass on God's forgiveness to those who have wronged me. Help me to look for ways to show kindness toward them. Thank you, Jesus, for loving me. I am glad that you are my friend.

It is time to say goodbye to Jesus....Get up and walk through the door....Turn and wave ....Walk down the path ....Open your eyes and come back into this room.

Discussion

- Do you think that Peter may have had a special reason for asking how many times he needed to forgive his brother? What was it?
- What is the real story Jesus told about?
- As a Christian, what is the most important thing to remember about forgiveness?

Jesus Is for Everyone

Scripture: Mk 10:13-16
Feast: Twenty-Seventh Sunday of Ordinary Time (B)
Music Suggestion: "Peace Is Flowing Like a River"/*Gentle Sounds*

Do you ever feel as though it is only older children or adults who get to do fun things? How often are you told, "Wait until you grow up" or "Wait until you are a little older." Once, when little children came to see Jesus, the disciples thought that Jesus was too busy to be bothered with children. Jesus saw them trying to keep the children away, but he had a different idea. Let's unzip our imaginations and see Jesus' different idea about the importance of children.

Meditation

Close your eyes....Take a deep breath....Let it out slowly.... Whisper "Jesus"....Relax....

You are standing in a field of tall grass....Look across the field....As far as you can see the blades of yellow-green grass blow in the summer wind....Small glimpses of color peek through the grass, flowers of red and yellow and tiny blue buttons....The air smells sweet from the blossoms.... Roll in the grass....Feel the sunshine on your back....Pick a dandelion....Blow the wisps of feathery petals into the air....Children are laughing....Some are playing tag....Some are throwing stones into the lake....There are many children playing in the field....This is the best of all days....

Your family wants Jesus to give you a blessing....There are so many people and so many children running around that you wonder how you will ever be able to see Jesus....There he is!....Stretch on your tip-toes, as high as you can go.... Jesus is standing on a hillside....Big people are gathered all around him....The sun in shining on his hair....You hear some of the adults grumbling....They are very grouchy today...."Quiet down!" one of them shouts....The red-haired man called Peter barks, "Stop that running around right now!"....How does that make you feel?....You feel sad and pushed aside, like sometimes when mom and dad are having a party and they send you off to bed early....Look up....Jesus is walking toward the hillside....He is taking long, fast strides....He does not see you....Instead he heads right for Peter and Andrew, the grouchy guys....Jesus speaks in a loud voice, "Let those children be. They are precious to me. I want always to hear their laughter".... Jesus is standing right in front of you....You can reach out and touch him....Jesus speaks to the adults, "I wish that you could all love me the way they do. I belong to everyone."

Jesus looks down at you and smiles....Jesus bends low and picks up a little baby girl....The baby gurgles and coos.... Placing the baby on the grass, Jesus joins a group of children dancing in a circle....Jesus invites you to join them ....Round and round you dance....Taking both of your hands, he swings you through the air....It feels as though you are flying....You are not afraid because you trust Jesus....Listen to Jesus laugh....Jesus kneels down on one knee and holds out his arms to you....Yes, you!....He wraps his arms about you and looks into your eyes....Jesus leans close and whispers, "Remember, I love you."

I will leave you alone with Jesus for some quiet time. Listen to his words....Tell Jesus what is on your heart.

Prayer

Jesus, thank you for being my friend. Surround me with your love. Help me to always trust in you....I know that you are here with me....I love you. Amen.

It is time to say goodbye to Jesus....Give Jesus a big hug.... Turn and walk away through the grassy field....Open your eyes and return to this room.

Discussion

- How did Jesus show that he loves children?
- What did Jesus mean when he said, "I belong to everyone"?
- Did you enjoy seeing Jesus laughing and playing? How can we show others our love of and trust in Jesus?

Activity

*Supplies: small ball of playdough or outline figure and markers for each child, candle, music tape "Oh, How I Love Jesus"/*Hi God 1

1. Give the children individual balls of playdough or a simple figure outline and markers and ask them to make small figures to represent themselves. When everyone is nearly finished, move the candle to the table, start the music, and turn off the lights. Ask the children to form a circle around the table. Explain to the children that Jesus is often called the "Light of the World" and that the candle is a reminder of Jesus' presence with us.

2. Ask each child to come forward with his or her figure. Invite the child to place the figure near the candle on the table, saying, "My name is (*Name*). I am a friend of Jesus." When every child has had a turn, keep the lights off and conclude with the Our Father.

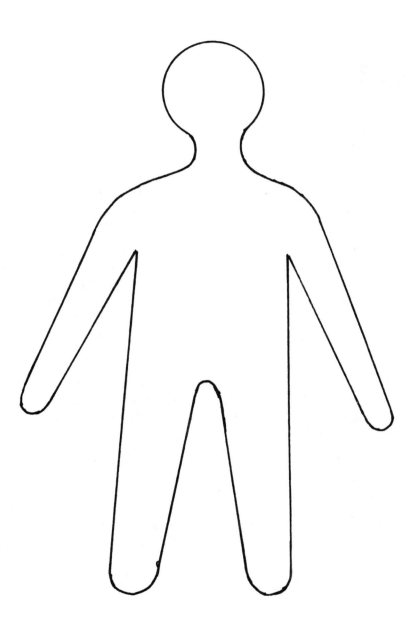

How to Follow Jesus

Scripture: Mt 19:16-30; Mk 10:17-27; Lk 18:18-30
Feast: Twenty-Eighth Sunday of Ordinary Time (B)
Music Suggestion: "By Name I Have Called You"/*Gentle Sounds*

Have you ever had to share something that you didn't want to share? How do you feel if your parent suggests that you share your favorite toy or clothing with a younger brother or sister? What if you were asked to share with a stranger? It is not always easy to share, is it? It is not easy either to always do the right thing. What does Jesus tell us about sharing?

Sometimes it is hard to be loving people. But if we want to be followers of Jesus, we have to learn how to do loving things even when sometimes we would rather not. Let's unzip our imaginations to be with Jesus when he asks a rich young girl to do something that was not easy.

Meditation

Close your eyes....Wiggle your toes....Take a deep breath ....Let it out slowly....Whisper "Jesus"....Relax....

It is a cool fall day....Leaves of gold and red blow across the road....Quick, step on a leaf!....Crunch....Crackle....The wind pulls gently on your hair....You are walking with Jesus and his friends....Jesus turns and looks at you....Smiling, he reaches out to catch a leaf blowing with the wind....He holds the crisp red leaf out in front of you, then releases.... Catch it!....Jesus takes your hand....You walk hand in hand down the winding road....

As you enter a small village a young girl runs up to Jesus, pushing you out of the way....The girl is dressed in her party clothes, with a fur coat with a hat to match....Her arms are loaded with expensive toys....More toys are loaded in a wagon behind her....You have never seen so many toys....The girl kneels down in front of Jesus...."Good teacher, what must I do to be happy?" she asks....Jesus picks up a small fur teddy bear, then looks down at the child....He speaks slowly, "You must keep the commandments of God"....The girl claps her hands, "I do keep all the commandments....I never, never steal, and I love God"....Jesus kicks the dirt with his toe...."My disciples know the commandments too. There are rules about how to live peacefully and how to love your neighbors and how to worship God. There are a lot of them, and it is not easy to keep them all"....Even this did not bother the girl....

"I have always obeyed all those commandments, even when I was very small," the girl boasts...."Then what is the problem?" Jesus asks. The girl bends her head, "I am still not happy. There must be something I can do"...."Well," Jesus speaks slowly, "There is one more thing you need to do....Go and sell everything you own. Give the money to the poor. Everyone in heaven shares. Then come and follow me. Come and be one of my disciples"....The girl looks shocked and very, very sad....She looks around at all of her toys and her pretty clothes, then mumbles, "Teacher, it is too hard to give away everything. I am very rich. I like all the things I have. I'm sorry. I cannot do what you ask".... The rich girl shakes her head, gathers up her toys, turns and slowly walks away....Jesus looks very sad and sighs.... He takes your hand in his and says, "Sometimes it is hard to do what God wants. Sometimes the choices are difficult and it seems impossible....But remember, my child, with God nothing is impossible"....Walk silently along with Jesus ....Jesus stops beside the village well....Leaning against the wall, he asks, "Do you think I was too hard on the girl?".... Jesus looks into your eyes, "Would you be willing to share everything you have? I know that it is very hard to share, but you can do it. I will help you."

I will leave you alone with Jesus to talk this over. Tell him what is on your heart.

Prayer
Jesus, help me to be like you. Help me to be kind. Help me to tell the truth. Help me to share. I ask this in your name, Jesus. Amen.

It is time to say goodbye....Give Jesus a hug....Turn and walk away....Open your eyes and return to this room.

Discussion

- Do you think the child in the story is a follower of Jesus? Why?
- Do you think that this was an easy choice to make?
- How do you think Jesus feels about the rich girl?
- What is Jesus really asking here?

One Comes Back

Scripture: Lk 17:11-19
Feast: Twenty-Eighth Sunday in Ordinary Time (C)
Music Suggestion: "Spirit of God"/*Instruments of Peace*
      OR "We Believe in You"/*Gentle Sounds*

What is the longest time you had to stay out of school because you were sick or hurt? Who took care of you? I bet the people taking care of you had to bring you meals in bed and perhaps even get up in the middle of the night. Did you thank them for taking good care of you? Do you find it difficult to write "thank you" notes? Sometimes we forget to say "thank you" to our families and even to God.

One day Jesus found out what it was like when people forget to say thank you. Jesus was on his way to Jerusalem when he encountered ten people who had leprosy. (*You may want to explain that untreated leprosy consists of open sores on the skin, often resulting in disfiguration. Leprosy is very contagious and people with leprosy were banned from entering the town and villages. They were completely rejected by the people.*) Let's unzip our imaginations, joining Jesus on the road between Galilee and Samaria.

Meditation

Close your eyes....Take a deep breath....Let it out slowly....
Whisper "Jesus"....Relax....

You are with Jesus and his disciples traveling down the
winding road between Galilee and Samaria....Dirt clouds
billow around your feet....The journey has been slow and
long....People hearing that Jesus is nearby flock to the
roadway, hoping to catch sight of him, often calling out for
Jesus to cure them....John, the youngest disciple, walks
beside you....Suddenly he points to a group of people
standing in the shade of a clump of trees....Look ahead....
There they are—men, women and two children near your
age....They are covered in rotting bandages....Peter warns,
"These people are lepers! Watch out!"....Look at the
children....Open sores cover their faces and hands....They
have dark circles under their eyes....They look hungry and
so sad....Mark places his hand on your shoulder, reassuring
you, "They won't bother us. It is against the law for them to
come near people"....The lepers huddle together, then one
of the lepers calls out to Jesus...."Jesus, help us. We really
are sick and you're the only one who can help us. If you
don't help us we will surely die"....Jesus walks to the edge
of the road....He looks with pity on the lepers, but he does
not walk toward them....You look up at Jesus....A tear falls
down his cheek...."Please, Jesus, help them," you whisper
to Jesus.....Jesus calls out to the lepers, "I'll help you, but
first go and show yourself to your priest"....Peter explains to
you, "According to the law priests are supposed to check
over people who have this kind of disease.The priests will
decide if they are healed"....

The ten lepers run toward the village....Jesus takes your
hand in his as you continue to make your way down the
dusty road....You walk in silence, thinking about what you
have just seen....As you walk through the village gate, two
men stand talking about the ten lepers. "I saw them with my

own eyes! They were all shouting, 'We are healed! We are healed!' Their skin is clear of sores"....Jesus smiles quietly to himself....A man runs toward you....He looks like one of the lepers....He is shouting and waving his arms....Quickly he comes to Jesus' side....The man, now straight and tall, falls to his knees, shouting praise and thanks to God.... "God is my strength. Thank you, Jesus, for making me whole again"....Jesus takes the man's hands in his, saying, "You are welcome, but weren't there ten people healed?" He turns to you and his disciples, asking, "Where are the other nine?" "Only one has come back," Peter growls.... Helping the man to his feet, Jesus speaks lovingly, "Stand up and go. Your faith has made you well"....The man slowly turns away, waving goodbye.

"That takes the cake. Only one bothers to tell Jesus thanks," mutters Peter....Jesus walks toward the village well ....His shoulders sag and sadness covers his face....Look down the road, then say to Jesus, "Maybe the others will return"....Jesus shakes his head, then turns to you, "Saying thanks is a way of worshiping God. Always be grateful for the things God does for you. God usually does things for us through other people. Always say 'Thank you.' God cares."

I will leave you alone with Jesus. Listen to what he wants to tell you. Spend some time thinking of all the gifts that God has given you.

Prayer
Jesus, Jesus, thank you for your love. Thank you for teaching me that God cares for our friends and for the people we don't like. God's love is for all of us; no one is outside the circle of God's love. Amen.

It is time for you to leave....Jesus gives you a hug....Turn and walk away....Open your eyes and return to this room.

Discussion

- Whom did Jesus meet on the way to Jerusalem?
- How many lepers were cured? How many came back to thank Jesus?
- Are there times when you act like an ungrateful leper?
- What do you think became of the grateful leper? Jesus told him to "Go on your way." What way was Jesus talking about?

Prayer Time

Invite the children to stand in a circle, extending hands with palms up for each response.

RESPONSE: Praise the Lord.

LEADER:

For the sunlight, butterflies, and colored leaves...

For puppy dogs, kittens, and animals to cuddle...

For Christmas, birthdays, and Easter...

For trees, flowers, picnics, and happy times...

For moms and dads, grandparents, friends, brothers and sisters...

For all you made, for loving everyone, for being a part of my life...

New Ways to Say "I Love You"

Scripture: Mt 22:34-40
Feast: Thirtieth Sunday of Ordinary Time (A)
Music Suggestion: "Peace Is Flowing Like a River"/*Gentle Sounds*

Do you have rules you must follow at home? Think for a moment about the one absolute rule that never, ever changes. (*List answers on chalkboard or newsprint.*) Are these rules always easy to follow? Of course they aren't, but Jesus is always there to help us. If you can't think of an important rule in your house, go home and talk about rules with your family.

What are some rules that God gave to us? The commandments, of course. Which one do you think is the most important of them all? One day a lawyer, thinking that he would trick Jesus, asked Jesus which of the commandments was the most important of them all. Jesus had a very simple answer for the young man and for us too. Let's unzip our imaginations, joining Jesus in the temple courtyard.

Meditation

Close your eyes....Wiggle your fingers one more time....
Take a deep breath....Let it out slowly....Whisper "Jesus"....
Relax....

You are with Jesus and his disciples in the temple courtyard
....Nearby an aged man calls out, "Doves for sale"....Many
people have gathered to hear Jesus speak and to question
him....Jesus motions for the crowd to quiet down....He sees
that you are almost being trampled by the crowd....Jesus
reaches toward you, offering you his hand....Pulling you to
his side, he says, smiling, "When I am finished we will go
someplace and talk....Wait right here for me"....Curl up on
a pillow next to Jesus' feet....

A young man steps in front of the crowd, raising his hand
to catch Jesus' attention...."Jesus, which is the greatest
commandment?" he asks. Jesus thinks for a moment, then
answers, "Love the Lord your God with your whole heart
and your whole mind and your whole soul. This is the first
and greatest commandment. And the second is like this:
Love your neighbor as you love yourself"....The man seems
puzzled by Jesus' answer, turning away....Jesus looks at you
saying, "Remember, my child, you cannot love God without
also loving your neighbor."

Jesus now steps down from the raised platform....Taking
your hand, he leads you to a bench near the fountain....The
water from the fountain reminds you of a gentle summer
rain...."Sit here, child," Jesus says, placing his hand on the
seat next to him....He offers you a cool drink of water from
the fountain....Take a long drink; enjoy the clear, cool
water...."I want you to remember that if you aren't able to
love a brother or sister you can see, then you may not be
able to love the God that we cannot see."

Jesus drapes his arm around your shoulders and, holding you close, he speaks, "Look into your heart and think of the times you may have forgotten to love your neighbor." Gazing at your reflection in the fountain, he asks, "My child, do you gossip about your friends? (*Pause briefly.*) Do you turn your head when you pass by the poor and homeless? (*Pause briefly.*) Do you forget to say, 'I love you'? (*Pause briefly.*) Think about this and then tell me how you can answer these questions"....I am going to leave you alone with Jesus for a moment. (*Pause for half a minute or until the children grow restless.*)

Prayer

Jesus, sometimes I do not show God's love toward others. I talk about my friends....I become angry....I forget to say, "I love you." Help me to love you with my whole heart, my whole mind, my whole soul, and to love my neighbors as myself. Amen.

It is time to say goodbye to Jesus....Give him a hug....Walk through the courtyard....Stop and wave goodbye....Open your eyes and come back to this room.

Discussion

- What did Jesus say is the most important commandment?
- What are some ways that we can show others that we love them?

Activity

Make small hearts to carry in pocket as a reminder to love one another.

Look to God for Healing

Scripture: Mk 10:46-52
Feast: Thirtieth Sunday in Ordinary Time (B)
Music Suggestion: "Healer of Every Ill"/*Instruments of Peace*
OR "When You Seek Me"/*Gentle Sounds*

Invite the children to spend a minute just looking around the room. Then ask them to close their eyes. Now give them some questions to think about.

What color is your sweater/shirt/blouse? Who is sitting on your right side? What color are his/her eyes? Who is missing from our class today? (*Invite them to open their eyes and share how they did and how they felt during the exercise.*) It must be very difficult to be blind. Sometimes we don't use our gift of sight well. We almost take it for granted. One day while Jesus was walking through the streets of a city, he noticed a young blind man begging for food. Once the blind man, called Bartimaeus, knew that Jesus was nearby, he never gave up trying to get Jesus' attention. Let's unzip our imaginations and join Jesus and the blind man who never gave up on Jesus.

Meditation

Close your eyes....Take a deep breath....Let it out slowly....
Put all the sounds that you hear out of your mind....Relax....

You are with Jesus and his disciples outside the city of
Jericho....Many people are on the road....Some push
empty carts to the marketplace....Others bring pigs and
lambs to sell....Children run ahead of their parents through
the gates of the city....Jesus takes your hand...."You must
be careful where you walk. This is a busy time of day,"
Jesus warns....Peter rushes ahead to a cart filled with fresh
fruits....He carefully chooses a bright red apple, then two,
then three....Returning to where you and Jesus stand, he
hands an apple to you and one to Jesus....James,
sometimes the dreamer, brings a bouquet of flowers from a
street vendor....Look at the flowers: red, yellow, and a
white daisy....This is truly a wonderful place to be....

Once through the gates of the city, you make your way
through the narrow cobblestone streets....Each building is
more beautiful than the last....Tall steeples reach toward the
heavens....You pass by a young man sitting on the edge of
the street....He begs for food....His clothes are in tatters....
He is thin and frail....You turn to tell Jesus about the blind
man, only to find that he has been nearly swallowed by the
gathering crowd....The blind man calls out, "What is going
on? Is there someone important here?"...."Jesus of
Nazareth is here," you inform him....The blind man calls
out to Jesus in a shrill voice, "Jesus, son of David, have
mercy on me!"....Jesus turns around, then calls you to his
side...."Who is that man?" he asks you....Before you can
answer, a woman from the town answers, "That is just
Bartimaeus. He is the town beggar. Don't pay any attention
to him"....You try to tug on Jesus' sleeve....Surely he will
notice you....But the crush of the crowd is too much....

A soldier in the crowd tells Bartimaeus to quiet down....But
the blind man calls out louder, "Son of David, have mercy
on me!" Jesus stops and once again asks you about this
man....Jesus smiles and sends you to bring Bartimaeus to
his side....Bend low, whisper in Bartimaeus' ear....Blind
Bartimaeus jumps up quickly, spilling his basket of

coins....Take his hand; it is thin and fragile, shaking with excitement....Lead Bartimaeus to Jesus' side.

Jesus reaches out, taking Bartimaeus' hands in his, "What do you want from me, my son?" he asks....Bartimaeus' eyes are clouded by blindness....He begs Jesus, "Grant that I may see the world with these eyes." Jesus looks squarely into eyes and announces, "I am the light of the world".... Bending down to the ground he mixes some saliva and dirt in his hand and makes mud out of it....Then he smears the mud over Bartimaeus' eyes....Jesus walks toward a fountain and washes his hands, telling Bartimaeus, "Come and wash the mud from your eyes"....Bartimaeus places his hand upon your shoulder....Lead him to the bubbling fountain.... Pour the cool waters into his waiting hands....When the last spot of mud is washed clean, Bartimaeus opens his eyes.

Bartimaeus' clouded eyes are now are a clear, bright blue.... "I can see! I can see!" he shouts in gladness....Jesus smiles at Bartimaeus....The crowd buzzes with excitement, crowding around Bartimaeus.

Jesus takes your hand and leads you away from the crowd ....Finding a small, fragrant garden, you sit on the lush green carpet of grass....The sweet smell of blossoms hangs in the air...."There is something I want you to understand," Jesus tells you....Sit closer to Jesus....He places his arm around your shoulders...."I was sent into this world to make people see not only with their eyes but also with their hearts. I have come so that others might see how to lead good lives"....Jesus looks deeply into your eyes, "Bartimaeus was healed because he had faith and trust in me. Do you believe that I love you?....Will you place your faith in me?"....Jesus bends low to hear your answer.

I will leave you in the garden with Jesus.

Prayer

Dear Jesus, sometimes I don't see your love all around me. Sometimes I don't understand what you want me to do. Allow me to see clearly and how to care and share with others. Amen.

It is time to tell Jesus goodbye....Walk down the garden path, past the rose bushes....Open your eyes and return to this room.

Discussion

- What did Bartimaeus do after he was healed?
- Do you have any friends or relatives with disabilities? Is life more difficult for them? Why or why not?
- How did Bartimaeus use his other senses to know about things?
- Why do you think Bartimaeus knew Jesus would heal him? What did Bartimaeus see with his eyes closed that the other people could not see?

The Funny Little Man

Scripture: Lk 19:1-10
Feast: Thirty-First Sunday of Ordinary Time (C)
Music Suggestion: "We Believe in You"/*Gentle Sounds*

Has anyone ever climbed a tree? I bet you could see the whole neighborhood from the top of the tree. When you were little, did you ever have trouble seeing through a crowd to watch a parade? Sometimes we are just a little too short to be able to see. Are you as tall as you would like to be? If you were ten inches taller, how would you feel? Sometimes we worry so much about how we look or what people think about us that we forget the important things. Growing closer to God is more important than how tall we are or how tall we are going to be.

One evening Jesus met a funny little short man called Zacchaeus. Zacchaeus had gone to a great deal of trouble to be able to see Jesus. Let's unzip our imaginations to be with Zacchaeus and Jesus when they first meet.

Meditation

Close your eyes....Wiggle your toes....Take a deep breath ....Let it out slowly....Whisper "Jesus"....Now, relax....

You are going through the gates of the city of Jericho.... Jesus takes your hand in his....The disciples are busy talking

166

among themselves....Jesus turns toward you and smiles, "I like this part of the day"....Jesus points toward the setting sun....The sky is filled with puffs of orange-streaked clouds....The blue sky of day peeks through the haze of color, holding onto the sunlight as long as possible....

Soon, a crowd begins to gather around Jesus, the disciples, and you....You are lost in the pressing crowd....You can't see Jesus....The disciple, Mark, tries to grab your hand but is shoved aside....You hear a man yelling, "Let me through. I must see Jesus"....At last, James makes his way to your side....He lifts you upon his shoulders....A funny looking little short man pushes through, yelling, "I can't see Jesus" ....He jumps up and down like a jack in the box....John, being much taller, clears a path for the little man dressed in purple....The man scurries through the crowd to a tall sycamore tree....Grasping the limbs of the tree, he pulls himself up into the tree, perching on a bough high above the street...."The man is a rich tax collector....The people don't like him....That's why they didn't let him through to see Jesus," James explains....James pushes through the milling crowd to Jesus' side....Jesus looks up at you, "How is the view from up there?" he asks, smiling....

Jesus stops under the sycamore tree, first looking around at the people, then glancing up and noticing Zacchaeus.... "Zacchaeus, come down out of that tree right now! I will stay at your house tonight"....The people do not like Jesus talking to Zacchaeus, murmuring, "That man is a sinner. How can Jesus stay with such a man?"....Zacchaeus hurriedly climbs down the tree....The short little man standing no taller than you stands open-mouthed in front of Jesus. His clothes are covered with tree bark....His right foot is bare, his toes twitching on the rocky road....The seat of his pants are ripped, showing much too much of his red underwear....You and the disciples begin to giggle at the sight....The corners of Jesus' mouth curve upward into a grin....Zacchaeus looks up at Jesus, "I know that I have done some bad things in my life, but now I want to make up for all those bad things. I will give half of all I have to the poor. And if I ever cheated anyone out of money, I will pay them back four times as much"....Jesus places his arm around Zacchaeus' shoulder as they walk toward Zacchaeus' home....The little man talks a mile a minute....Jesus occasionally nods his head. Through a grove of trees you catch glimpse of the largest house you have ever seen.

Zacchaeus invites everyone into his home....Beautiful gardens surround the large pink house....Zacchaeus' chubby body jiggles like Jell-O as he rushes about making plans for his guests....Zacchaeus' excitement fills the house...."Me! My house! I can't believe that Jesus is eating dinner with me!" he exclaims....Look about you at all the riches, the house, jewelry, furniture, servants, beautiful gardens, pools....Catching up with Zacchaeus, you ask, "How can you give all this up?"....Zacchaeus stops momentarily, "I have been touched by God. I will find new life in following the man Jesus"....Zacchaeus hurries off to the kitchen.

Jesus, knowing the questions on your heart, takes you by the hand....You and Jesus walk toward the garden.... "Zacchaeus wants to change his life and grow closer to me. Zacchaeus will be less concerned about himself and more concerned about the needs of others," Jesus says softly.... Jesus bends low and, looking into your eyes, he speaks, "Do you want to grow closer to me? I will show you the way."

Take this time to be alone with Jesus. Talk this over with Jesus. Look into your heart.

Prayer
*Jesus, help me to grow closer to you. May I be
willing to change as Zacchaeus did. I love you.
Thank you for being my friend.*

It is time to leave Jesus in the garden. Give Jesus a hug. Say goodbye for now. Begin to walk through the garden gate.... Open your eyes and return to this room.

Discussion

- Why did Zacchaeus want to see Jesus? (*Point out that it may have just been curiosity at first.*)
- What did Jesus say to Zacchaeus? How did Zacchaeus respond to Jesus?
- What are some ways we can grow closer to Jesus?

■ Music Resources

Good music for guided meditations is readily available from both religious and secular stores. Listen for music that can set a mood, usually peaceful, but does not call attention to itself. This is the kind of music that you might put on for a quiet dinner or to create a relaxing environment. This is not children's music, by and large, but much of it will work fine for this purpose. Here are some of my personal favorites.

Arkenstone, David. *Another Star in the Sky.* Narada Music.

Darnell, Dik. *Ceremony.* Etherean Music. Beautiful instrumentals that work well with the meditations.

Haugen, Marty. *Instruments of Peace.* GIA. You may need to be more selective about music choice for each meditation.

Hi God 1. NALR.

Hi God 2. NALR.

In the Spirit We Belong. Canadian Conference of Catholic Bishops.

Landry, Carey. *Gentle Sounds.* NALR. This album works very well with the meditations. The music is arranged so that you are able to cross from one piece to the next without disrupting the meditation.

We Belong to God. Canadian Conference of Catholic Bishops.

Winston, George. *December.* Windham Hill Productions.

Cycle A

Advent & Christmas

Lent & Easter

Ordinary Time

Cycle B

Advent & Christmas

Lent & Easter

Ordinary Time

Cycle C

Advent & Christmas

Lent & Easter

Ordinary Time